RONALD REAGAN

other titles in the **BIOGRAPHY**® *book series:*

Jacqueline Kennedy Onassis

Pope John Paul II

Muhammad Ali

RONALD REAGAN

Kenneth T. Walsh

A Balliett & Fitzgerald Book

PARK LANE

NEW YORK

For Barclay—KTW

This 1997 edition is published by Park Lane Press,
a division of Random House Value Publishing, Inc.,
a Random House Company
201 East 50th Street, New York, New York 10022

A&E's acclaimed BIOGRAPHY series is available on video cassette
from A&E Home Video. Call 1-800-423-1212 to order.

A&E and **BIOGRAPHY** are trademarks of A&E Television Networks,
registered in the United States and other countries.

Park Lane Press and colophon are trademarks of
Random House Value Publishing, Inc.

Random House
New York • Toronto • London • Sydney • Auckland
http://www.randomhouse.com/

Printed and bound in the United States of America

A Balliett & Fitzgerald Book
Series Editor: Thomas Dyja
Book Design: Lisa Govan, Susan Canavan
Copy Editor: William Drennan
Photo Research: Maria Fernandez
and special thanks to Judy Capadanno, Bill Huelster,
and John Groton at Random House

Library of Congress Cataloging-in-Publication Data

Walsh, Kenneth T.
    Ronald Reagan : Biography / Kenneth T. Walsh
            p.   cm.   — (Biographies from A&E)
    Includes bibliographical references.
    1. Reagan, Ronald. 2. Presidents—United States—
Biography. 3. Governors—California—Biography. 4. Motion
picture actors and actresses—United States—Biography.
I. Title. II. Series.
E877.W34 1997
973.928'092—dc20
(B)   96-36063
                                                     CIP

ISBN 0-517-20078-3
10 9 8 7 6 5 4 3 2 1
First Edition

CONTENTS

———◆———

circa 1913

CHAPTER ONE

MIDDLE AMERICAN

Only one dusty thoroughfare cut through the small town of Tampico, Illinois, in 1911, but Main Street was still the focal point of commerce in this farm-oriented corner of northwestern Illinois. The automobile was largely a novelty; most people traveled by horse or train, and the daily routine was simple: Folks got up at dawn to work on their farms or in their shops or to hire themselves out for manual labor for ten or twelve hours. They would come home for supper, gossip some, then retire early. The world revolved around family, friends, and the seemingly eternal verities of hard work, optimism, and patriotism.

This was the America into which Ronald Reagan was born on February 6, 1911, a nation of relative innocence and simplicity. Reagan's father, John Edward "Jack" Reagan, explained that he gave the nickname "Dutch" to his newborn son because the infant looked like "a little bit of a fat

Dutchman." In 1914 Jack Reagan moved his wife, Nelle, along with Dutch and his older son, Neil, from Tampico to Chicago, where Jack briefly worked as a clerk at the large Marshall Field's department store. The family proceeded to move through several small Illinois towns until finally, in December 1920, they settled in Dixon, a small, agricultural community in northwestern Illinois that is just twenty-five miles from Tampico. Jack Reagan was to be a partner in the Fashion Boot Shop. Dutch was nine years old at the time, and from then on he considered rough-edged, predominantly working-class Dixon his hometown.

In many ways it was a pleasant existence, but hardly as idyllic as the future president would later portray it in speeches and in writings. The Reagan family differed from most others in the area. They were Democrats in a Republican region, and Jack Reagan was a Catholic amid Protestants. Jack was also an alcoholic. Ronald recalls in his autobiography that at age eleven, he found his father passed out—"drunk, dead to the world" and reeking of liquor—on the front porch of their modest home. He reports matter-of-factly that he dragged his dad inside and helped him into bed. Although incidents like this occurred with considerable frequency, the family had extraordinary tolerance for Jack's lapses, largely born from Nelle's belief that alcoholism was a sickness, not a character flaw. Still, even with Nelle's forbearance, Jack's drinking put a constant strain on their marriage and exacerbated the differences between his outgoing, erratic nature and her deeply held faith in a religion based on temperance and restraint.

Like many family members of alcoholics, Reagan began at a young age to put a good face on bad times and avoid personal confrontation. Young Dutch was known as a dreamer, a boy whose bad eyesight made such quiet pastimes as playing with toy soldiers and examining bugs his favorite diversions. While his brother Neil took more after his father, Dutch tended to spend more time with his mother.

Nelle Reagan was Scots-Irish and "a natural practical do-gooder," as Reagan would later recall. The greatest influence on her life was her membership in the Christian Church. Mrs. Reagan taught her two sons that people should care for one another, a belief that bred in Reagan the principle and faith that Americans' charitable instincts would take over in times of need, that government was not required to provide welfare or other services. She would give dramatic readings to prisoners in local jails, and sometimes even allow newly released ex-convicts to sleep in the sewing room until they could find another place to stay. Even though business was tough in Dixon and the cost of living high, Nelle tithed 10 percent of the family's income to the Christian Church.

One thing that Nelle did share with Jack was a dramatic bent. She belonged to the local drama group and felt that the theater was a reasonable vehicle for dealing with personal issues. Historian Garry Wills reports a story told him by a woman who had known Nelle. The woman had recently had a fight with her husband that the entire congregation knew about. Nelle requested the couple attend the next theatrical, at which she presented a brief play on family fights, starring herself as the mother and Dutch as the father. Many in the church believed that with a better education, Nelle Reagan would have made a great preacher. Though both sons were baptized into the church in 1922, Dutch was the more active of the two and enjoyed participating in Nelle's dramatic performances. Nelle and Dutch grew closer through these shared times.

Nelle Reagan also valued common sense, and despite the nativist slant of her religion, she taught her boys to judge people as individuals. One reason for her open-mindedness was that she understood the discrimination that her Catholic husband had endured—and resented—all his life. Nelle also pushed her sons to improve themselves and, like many Americans, she attempted to instill in them a belief in education, including college, as a ticket toward a better life. "Many folks reasoned, maybe the children weren't worth the $3,600 investment and the four years thrown away when a man could be out on a real job," Ronald wrote later. She quickly succeeded with Dutch, but Neil would not become a believer in education until his younger brother led the way by enrolling in Eureka College years later; Neil would eventually give up his job as a laborer and follow suit.

❧ ❧ ❧

"I'm a sucker for hero worship."

Despite his drinking problem, Jack Reagan managed to keep his family supplied with the necessities of life, and Dutch always remembered him with fondness. Perhaps it was because, drinking aside, the son reflected the father in many ways. Jack could be a charming man, handsome and easygoing, a raconteur and a die-hard Democrat. He taught Dutch and Neil that "all men were created equal and [a] man's own ambition determines what happens to him. . . ." Jack forbade his sons to see the film *The Birth of a Nation* because it was racist. Once, when the boys were older, he refused to stay in a hotel that did not permit Jews to take rooms; Jack told the clerk, "I'm a Catholic, and if it's come to a point where you won't take Jews, you won't take Catholics." He slept in his car for the night and got sick; family members felt that the incident weakened him so much that he caught pneumonia and soon had a heart attack. All this imbued a spirit of decency in the young Ronald Reagan that would later prevent him from exhibiting the sort of personal vitriol common in political life. Friends said his family had been sufficiently unorthodox that he could tolerate unconventional views or behavior in other people. Regardless of the often harsh social policies he came to espouse as a politician, his upbringing gave him an affable tolerance on a one-to-one level that he never lost.

When Reagan was young, there were still men in his community who had fought in the Civil War a half-century earlier, and he revered them. "I'm a sucker for hero worship," he once said later in his life. As a boy he was well aware that one of his heroes, Ulysses S. Grant, had risen from failure, drunkenness, and ridicule to lead his nation to victory over the Confederacy and later to win the presidency. That, in Reagan's mind, was what America was all about—a boy could grow up to be whatever he wanted, and even a drunken failure had a chance to be president. One of his favorite books as a child was *That Printer of Udell's* by Harold Bell Wright, in which a Horatio Alger-type hero rises from printer to successful businessman, in the process combining Christian principles with free enterprise and good luck. ". . . [M]y reading left an abiding belief in the triumph of good over evil," Reagan recalled. "There were heroes who lived by standards of morality and fair play." Throughout his youth, Reagan would attach himself to father figures, creating heroes when his father was unable to fill that role.

With all this emphasis on heroes and his charged religious upbringing, Reagan was able to push through the complexities of his family life and grasp onto the security offered by a clear-cut concept of right and wrong—a quintessentially American attitude encouraged by the leaders of the Christian Church and no one less than the chief executive of the United States. When the nation went to war on April 6, 1917, President Woodrow Wilson issued his call to arms by exhorting Congress: "... [T]he right is more precious than peace, and we shall fight for the things which we have always carried nearest our hearts—for democracy, for the right of those who submit to authority to have a voice in their own governments, for the rights and liberties of small nations, for a universal dominion of right by such a concert of free peoples as shall bring peace and safety to all nations, and make the world itself at last free."

Morality and fair play are, of course, relative; Reagan's critics, for example, would later attack him for currying favor with a small band of rich, right-wing Californians who would bankroll his political career. Where, the critics asked, was the fair play in that? There was also an insularity to this vision of America. Reagan recalled in his autobiography the coming of the 1918 armistice, which ended World War I when he was seven years old. He wrote, "I think the realization that some of those boys to whom I'd waved on the troop train later died on European soil made me an isolationist for a long time." Always discomfited by that outside world, Reagan was brought up to consider America a promised land that needed to be kept safe from corrupting or polluting influences, especially, after World War II ended, the evil of communism.

Sixty years later, Reagan loved to begin political speeches by talking about two boys, one an optimist and one a pessimist. Their parents wanted to give the downbeat child reason for hope, and confront the upbeat child with the negative side of life, so they locked the pessimist in a room with new toys and the optimist in a room filled with horse manure. The pessimistic child began weeping in frustration; he refused to play with the toys out of fear that he might break one. The optimistic child cheerfully began shoveling out the room. "With this much manure around," he chirped, "I know there's a pony in here someplace."

Reagan always forced himself to look for that pony.

❧ ❧ ❧

"Life is just one grand, sweet song. . ."

By 1924 the Fashion Boot Shop had failed to keep the Reagans above water, let alone make Jack's fortune, so the Reagans had moved to a lesser house, which Nelle bravely decorated. Dutch entered Northside High, while Neil went to Southside High School, known as a rougher, more sports-oriented school. Located in the nicer part of town, Northside was focused more on culture. The differences between the schools attended by the boys pointed up the differences within the family—Neil and Jack on one side, Dutch and Nelle on the other—and the Reagan household became more polarized. A tense but ultimately still friendly competition emerged between Dutch and his brother, though at age thirteen, Ronald could hardly seem like a threat to steal much more than his mother's love. Short, skinny, wearing thick, horn-rimmed glasses, Dutch was nothing special. His myopia kept him from playing baseball—he could rarely see the pitches as they came near the plate—but he threw himself into football, first as a tackle and then as a guard, both positions where nearsightedness is less of a problem. Eventually

Ronald Reagan, in the horn-rimmed glasses on the left in the top row, poses for a photograph with the Northside High School student council.

he made the varsity team. He was an average student, but brother Neil and friends recalled that he had an excellent memory. He could read his school assignments just before an exam and retain the information indefinitely—a skill that let him memorize scripts in Hollywood with considerable ease and, later, deliver speeches effectively after only a rehearsal or two.

Dutch became a personality in Dixon when he took a job as lifeguard in his junior year, working twelve hours, seven days a week during summers and notching seventy-seven lives saved in a log near his station. It was here that he finally caught the eye of Margaret "Mugs" Cleaver, the daughter of Reverend Ben Cleaver, the minister of the Dixon Christian Church that the Reagans belonged to. Mugs was a classmate at Northside. Reagan's infatuation finally became a romance that would last through college. Though Mugs dated other boys, in senior year she went out with only Reagan, and the church expected them to marry directly after high school.

Combined with Jack Reagan's use of the well-told tall tale, Dutch's exposure to Nelle's staged dramatic performances had developed in him a strong interest in the theater. Reagan's other great influence in high school was his English and history teacher B. J. Frazier, who encouraged Dutch to join the drama club. Frazier was the adviser to the drama club at Northside and was unusual for his time and place for staging serious plays at the school. With Frazier's support, Reagan's interest became love after he shared the stage with Margaret Cleaver as the leads in the school's production of the Philip Barry play *You and I*. The experience made him more popular at school and proved to him that he could excel off the football field. After playing Ricky, the young son in *You and I*, and then the villain in *Captain Applejack*, he learned that "heroes are more fun."

Reagan's dramatic abilities were born in the same place as his gift for embellishment. From his days as a sports announcer who invented events to fill time, to the Hollywood actor who reinvented himself for each role he played, it was always difficult for Reagan to separate the worlds of fantasy and reality; he knew that if he believed what he was saying at the moment, his sincerity would show through and make him all the more persuasive. And maybe it even would become the truth itself. If he believed everything was fine between Nelle and Jack, maybe it really would be. As self-delusional as it

LIFEGUARD

Lean, strong, and a powerful swimmer, the teenaged Ronald Reagan spent seven summers working at Lowell Park, a three-hundred-acre recreation area at the Rock River and Dam near his hometown of Dixon, Illinois. Starting in 1926, when he was fifteen years old, he made $15 a week, saving most of it for college. When he got to Hollywood years later, the legend spread that at Lowell Park he had tried to save pretty young girls when they were in no danger of drowning, just to introduce himself. Reagan denied this, with a twinkle in his eye. The most important part of the experience was what it taught him about human nature.

"Lifeguarding provides one of the best vantage points in the world to learn about people," Reagan wrote in his autobiography. "During my career at the park, I saved seventy-seven people. I guarantee you they needed saving—no lifeguard gets wet without good reason. . . . Not many thanked me, much less gave me a reward, and being a little money-hungry I'd done a little daydreaming about this. They felt insulted.

"I got to recognize that people hate to be saved: Almost every one of them later sought me out and angrily denounced me for dragging them to shore. 'I would have been fine if you'd let me alone,' was their theme. 'You made a fool out of me trying to make a hero out of yourself.' "

In his mind, the lesson in laissez-faire applied just as much to politics and government as it did to recreational swimming: People want to take care of themselves, and it wounds their pride and makes them resentful when someone intervenes to "save" them.

As a lifeguard, he concluded, what he needed to do was simply "watch for the unexpected but keep my eye mainly on the two or three places where trouble would begin. . . ."

may seem, it also allowed Reagan to adapt to and survive a rocky childhood, a painful divorce, and a disappointing Hollywood career. In later years he came to understand that the chief function of leadership, at least presidential leadership, was essentially to serve as a national storyteller: to develop a positive vision of America and what it means to the world, and connect that vision to the past, present, and future.

In his senior year, a growth spurt pushed Dutch to his adult height of nearly six feet and he gained 30 pounds, weighing in at 165. He became a solid, competitive football player, and his love for the sport continued all his life. "It is the last thing left in civilization where two men can literally fling themselves bodily at one another in combat and not be at war," he once explained. "It's a kind of clean hatred. . . . I know of no other game that gave me the same feeling football did. That's why you can look at the bench when the TV camera comes over and see the fellows there crying. I've sat there crying." Reagan was elected student body president in his senior year at Northside, only reinforcing the Panglossian optimism that he put forward. The motto under his name in the school yearbook of 1928, his senior year, read: "Life is just one grand, sweet song, so start the music."

❦ ❦ ❦

"I have found it."

During a Eureka College homecoming rally on October 17, 1980, Ronald Reagan said, "As far as I am concerned, everything good that has happened to me—everything—started here on this campus in those four years that still are such a part of my life."

Indeed, Reagan always treasured his college years, and the

experience was formative for him. Within the small and secure confines of Eureka College, twenty-one miles east of Peoria, Illinois, he became conscious of his limitations; while he was neither an intellectual who excelled easily in his studies nor a first-class athlete who dominated the football field, Reagan found he could make his mark as a persuader, a performer, and a man who persevered. This was knowledge he would put to use as he pursued a radio career and later turned to movies, television, and politics.

He chose Eureka College, affiliated with the Christian Church, because one of his boyhood idols, high school fullback Garland Waggoner, went there. Waggoner was the son of a local minister, and Reagan hoped to follow in his tracks. Margaret Cleaver, Reagan's high school sweetheart, also planned to attend, which sealed his decision, despite the enormous financial hardships college would present.

He enrolled in 1928, joining a student body of 130 boys and 120 girls. Eureka—Greek for "I have found it"—gave Reagan an athletic scholarship for his swimming and football talents. The scholarship paid $90 of his $180 annual tuition and part of his board. The arrangement required him to wash dishes in a fraternity house and later in a girls' dormitory. Meanwhile, the $400 he had saved from his summers as a lifeguard helped pay for his lodging. During his junior and senior years he earned his board as a lifeguard at the college's swimming pool and also served as Eureka's swimming coach.

He also began to exhibit modest leadership skills. As a freshman he participated in a student strike, organized by the faculty, to protest new Eureka College president Bert Wilson's proposal to eliminate various courses and lay off faculty members to balance the school's budget. He would find himself on the opposite end of student protests when he was governor of

California many years later, but this was hardly the kind of angry and sometimes violent protest he later railed against. According to Reagan, most students simply stayed away from classes while the instructors took role, marked everyone present, and returned home. It was wintertime, so the students engaged in various winter sports, only breaking for a daily afternoon dance sponsored by the strike committee and basketball practice.

"Not once did we neglect our studies," Reagan said. "To have done so would have been to contradict the whole spirit of what we were fighting for. The committee set up regular study hours and enforced them: we concocted our own assignments and worked them out (and in some cases were ahead of the regular study schedule). . . . The publicity helped, but in the end it was our policy of polite resistance that brought victory." A week later, Bert Wilson resigned and the school returned to normal, with the faculty, on whose behalf the students had joined the strike, promising no new salary demands to ease the budget pressures.

This account, written in Reagan's autobiography in 1965 as he was preparing to run for governor of California, was intended to humanize him with voters while also showing that his own experience as a student protester was more responsible and less frivolous than that of protesters in the sixties. But serving as the freshman representative on the strike committee not only made Reagan a hero on campus, it also furthered his sense that drama could be a powerful force and that he was good at it. During one speech he gave in the Eureka chapel to the strike committee, he recalled, "Giving that speech—my first—was as exciting as any I ever gave. For the first time in my life, I felt my words reach out and grab an audience, and it was exhilarating. When I'd say something, they'd roar after every sentence, sometimes every word, and after a while, it was as if the audience and I were one."

The naive atmosphere on campus, where Reagan had pledged for the Tau Kappa Epsilon fraternity, also shaped Reagan's quaint sense of sexual morality, though he was hardly a prude. A handsome and glib fellow, he was popular with the girls and enjoyed the practice of "kegging"—the name given on campus for a romantic picnic supper outdoors. After dances in the gym and at fraternity houses, Reagan would sometimes neck at a nearby cemetery, a favorite spot of the college crowd.

Reagan showed another form of social liberalism in those days: racial tolerance. It had nothing to do with ideology or political activism and everything to do with the kind of fair play his parents had advocated as well as Reagan's sense of loyalty to those in his circles. Reagan also credited his participation in team sports and the exposure it provided him to African Americans for what he considered his enlightened views. He believed that among all those he felt to be causing racial strife in the mid-sixties, black or white, none had ever participated in a sport on an integrated team. He played football for Eureka beside Franklin "Burky" Burghardt, the starting center and an African American. During one trip, the team was to stay overnight near Dixon and work out on Reagan's old high school field, but when the time came to check into a local hotel, the owner would not allow Burky and another African-American player, named Jim Rattan, to rent rooms. Eureka coach Ralph McKinzie decided that the entire team would sleep on the bus rather than submit the two black players to this humiliation. Dutch Reagan came up with a solution: He would take the two African Americans home with him for the night, and the white players would stay at the hotel. In welcoming the black players, Nelle and Jack Reagan "didn't even blink or act as if anything had happened that was not a daily occurrence," Reagan later said.

❧   ❧   ❧

"... to close down a bureaucracy ..."

The sweet song that Dutch had sung leaving high school ended with the onset of the Depression. The economic collapse, along with his drinking, cost Jack Reagan his stake in the Fashion Boot Shop by 1929. It also sent Nelle Reagan to work in a dress shop and forced Ronald, by then at Eureka College, to work part-time so he could send his mother (without his father's knowledge) $50 a month, extending her credit at a local grocery store. For a period during Reagan's college years, his parents temporarily separated, Jack going to Springfield, Illinois, to work briefly at another shoe store. The reason given was finances, but it is possible that personal issues also led to the short break. According to Reagan, on Christmas Eve 1931 Jack received a letter telling him that he had been fired from his next job, as a traveling salesman. For all his faults, Jack Reagan did not give up; he worked for Franklin D. Roosevelt's presidential campaign in 1932, and when Roosevelt won, he was placed in charge of the local welfare office. While Ronald was in college, his father handed out food and the scrip used then as food stamps. Ronald would sometimes sit with his dad in the relief office and watch the sad procession of embarrassed neighbors get their handouts. In his second autobiography, he recalled with approval that even President Roosevelt, father of the New Deal, said "Government giveaway programs. . . 'destroy the human spirit.'" Writing in 1990, Reagan went on to say "As smart as he was, though, I suspect even FDR didn't realize that once you created a bureaucracy, it took on a life of its own. It was almost impossible to close down a bureaucracy once it had been created."

The Reagan family was relatively lucky; both parents were employed through the worst of the Depression. Yet Ronald could never forget how close his family and their community had come to disaster. Reagan was grateful to Roosevelt for helping many Americans, including his father, survive the Depression, and Roosevelt became another one of his heroes. He listened to the president's optimistic "fireside chats," memorized passages of FDR's first inaugural address, and did a passable imitation of him. Throughout his life Reagan retained his devotion to FDR's sense of drama, uplift, and confidence, but the big government that resulted from FDR's policies eventually became Reagan's greatest target. Reagan emerged from the Depression, like so many other Americans alive then, with financial security as the fundamental goal of his professional life.

❧ ❧ ❧

"Ye did great, ye big S.O.B.!"

After majoring in economics and sociology, Reagan graduated from Eureka in 1932. As his interest in acting had increased in college, he had joined the dramatic society and

FDR & THE NEW DEAL

FRANKLIN DELANO ROOSEVELT, CIRCA 1936.

Though it may now seem odd that Reagan considered Franklin D. Roosevelt a hero, in fact FDR's nomination acceptance speech to the Democratic National Convention in 1932 called for a balanced budget and a lean government. Only after his election did he begin to use the federal government in unprecedented ways to reduce the nation's suffering during the Depression and, later, to transform national life.

During his first hundred days in office, in early 1933, FDR persuaded Congress to enact a variety of sweeping proposals, creating public-works and relief programs, reforming the banking system, setting up the Tennessee Valley Authority, liberalizing farm credit, and legalizing the sale of alcoholic beverages. In 1935 he created Social Security, which for the first time provided a safety net of federal insurance for the unemployed and the elderly.

He went on to enact programs to help many of those least able to help themselves, such as fatherless children and the handicapped. His National Labor Relations Act of 1935 ensured workers the right to form unions, and the Civilian Conservation Corps employed thousands of young people on conservation projects. He strengthened the federal government's powers to regulate the economy, from banking and securities to aviation and fair labor practices. Within a decade, his New Deal had transformed American society. Most voters were persuaded that the federal government could—and should—play an activist role in solving the country's problems. The New Deal also revolutionized American politics. Uniting behind Roosevelt and the Democratic Party was a disparate coalition that included city dwellers, farmers, Catholics, Jews, union members, Southerners, blacks, and liberals. This coalition became a governing majority that gave Roosevelt four terms and allowed the Democrats to dominate national politics, with some exceptions, until the 1950s.

enrolled in a theater course. In his junior year he had won an award in the annual Eva Le Gallienne Competition for one-act plays at Northwestern University's School of Speech. Reagan played a Greek shepherd boy who is strangled during Edna St. Vincent Millay's *Aria da Capo*. "No actor can ask for more," he wrote. "Dying is the way to live in the theater." Seeing so many people out of work during the Depression convinced Reagan that the safe paths offered no more security than aiming high. He was certain that he wanted to pursue a career in sports, drama, or politics, and he showed little interest in his grades. He would not be tempted to follow the conventional route toward a teaching position or some other such everyday job. Aiming high would be his only choice. Margaret, to whom he was unofficially engaged, was skeptical. Though he had made the college football team more on his enthusiasm than his talent, sports was unlikely. He decided to give radio a try.

Radio had entered the homes of America in the early twenties, going from one station in 1920 to 556 in only three years. Many initially thought it would prove to be just another fad in a time particularly taken with them, but the surge continued on through the decade. In 1923, Edwin Howard Armstrong, one of the premier inventors of radio technology, installed an antenna for the Radio Corporation of America atop New York's Aeolian Hall. Ten years later RCA had built a massive skyscraper in Rockefeller Center, its huge neon "RCA" glowing over New York City. For the first time, all of America could simultaneously experience and share news and sports events and entertainment, and America couldn't get enough of the experience.

Although the radio industry suffered like every other business in the Depression, it remained an especially attractive one for a young man. The jobs were still new and full of untried challenges, and considering that there were now nearly twenty million radios across America, a person with energy and vision could make a good living and even become famous in the process. Freshly minted from Eureka College, Reagan hitchhiked a hundred miles to Chicago and made the rounds of the radio networks. He was turned away at NBC, CBS, and several local stations he had looked up in the telephone book. A kindly secretary finally took pity on him and offered some advice: Try smaller stations in "the sticks" to get some experience. Reagan agreed and hitchhiked back home to Dixon, Illinois.

He got lucky at WOC—named for "World of Chiropractic"—a station founded by Colonel B. J. Palmer of the Palmer School of Chiropractic in Davenport, Iowa, sixty miles from home. Reagan met Peter MacArthur, a native of Scotland and former vaudevillian who was being treated for arthritis at the Palmer School and was program director at WOC. A job as announcer had been filled the week before Reagan showed up in MacArthur's office, but the eager young applicant mentioned that he was also interested in sports announcing.

"Do ye think ye could tell me about a game and make me see it?" MacArthur asked in his Scottish burr. "I mean, really see it, so as I'd know what was goin' on?"

"I think I could," Reagan replied.

Moments later he found himself before a microphone for a test. He decided to re-create a Eureka College game in which he had played the previous autumn against Western State University, a game which Eureka won, 7–6, on a last-moment touchdown and point after. Reagan recounted the final heroics not just as he remembered them but also as he wished them to be, all for dramatic effect. In the actual game, Reagan had missed his blocking assignment on the key play, but his teammate was still able to manage a sixty-five-yard touchdown run. In his audition for MacArthur, he made the key block; it made the broadcast that much better—and secured his future as a radio announcer.

"Ye did great, ye big S.O.B.!" MacArthur said afterward. Reagan was hired to do the play-by-play for four University of Iowa football games.

It took a bit of dramatic license, but he was on his way in show business, and the combination of perseverance and serendipity that gave him his start reinforced his belief that in America all things are possible.

Then he was fired because he was unpersuasive in reading the commercials. He would admit later in his acting career that he was always terrible, despite his impressive memory, at first reads and especially so in those early days at WOC. When his replacement arrived, the new man demanded a contract to preserve his job security. WOC refused to provide one, and Reagan was rehired immediately. From then on, he began to rehearse as much as possible, a lesson he never forgot.

As one dream started, another one came to an end. Margaret Cleaver went to France for a year in 1933, and in 1934 Reagan received a letter from her explaining that she was getting married to a man she had met while overseas. Reagan took the breakup hard, buying a new car to cheer himself up. His situation didn't improve when Jack Reagan had a heart attack, forcing Dutch to help support the family along with Neil, whom he had gotten a job at WOC. Reagan bore down and quickly got the knack of radio, achieving by the mid-thirties a considerable degree of fame and financial security, his mellifluous voice known to millions throughout the Midwest. He went on to broadcast the home baseball games of the Chicago Cubs and Chicago White Sox for WOC and its sister station, WHO in Des Moines. He followed the practice of the day, re-creating the games as they happened as he sat in a studio in Davenport, 150 miles from the ballpark, reading telegraph accounts of each play sent to him by Morse code. Reagan would embellish the terse play-by-play sent over the wire with his own patter, describing the action as if he were an eyewitness.

During one game between the Cubs and the St. Louis Cardinals, the telegraph line went dead in the ninth inning of a scoreless tie, with Dizzy Dean pitching for the Cards and Augie Galan at bat for Chicago. Ad-libbing, Reagan had Galan foul off pitches for the next six minutes and forty-five seconds, and described in time-consuming detail where the fictitious balls landed and how the fans scrambled to retrieve them as souvenirs. When the connection was restored, Reagan found out that Galan had popped out on the first pitch.

He would tell that story innumerable times over the years. It never bothered him that he had merged fantasy and reality to deceive his listeners (sometimes when he told it, Galan was at bat; at other times, Billy Jurges); the idea was to put on an interesting show and make people feel good—essential ingredients, he felt, of the entertainment game.

By the mid-thirties Reagan was ready to get out of radio. He'd moved farther and farther away from Dixon, and now it was time to head west, to Hollywood.

circa 1940

CHAPTER TWO

ACTOR

———————◆———————

Every year the Chicago Cubs went to Catalina Island, off the coast of Southern California, for spring training. Given that one of Reagan's jobs as a sportscaster was to give insider information to his listeners, Dutch argued to WHO management that he should be sent for the 1937 preseason stint. His real reason had nothing to do with baseball: Reagan's goal was to be "discovered" by Hollywood. A former WHO personality in Des Moines, Joy Hodges, who was then a singer in Los Angeles, made the arrangements for him to meet her agent. An up-and-coming young actor under contract to Warner Brothers had recently committed suicide, and the studio needed someone to fill that position. Seeing the opening, Hodges's agent, George Ward, of the Meiklejohn Agency, pitched Reagan as the next Robert Taylor, and Warner's jumped on the chance to give him a screen test. Reagan performed a scene from Philip Barry's *Holiday*, then headed back to Des Moines without waiting to see how the screen test went.

25

Though he felt optimistic about what he'd done in Hollywood, he immediately regretted leaving so quickly, thinking he might have blown his shot at the movies. His first day back in Des Moines he received a telegram from Bill Meiklejohn, the agent who had escorted him to the studios. "WARNER'S OFFER CONTRACT SEVEN YEARS, ONE YEAR'S OPTIONS, STARTING AT $200 A WEEK. WHAT SHALL I DO? MEIKELJOHN."

Reagan replied: "HAVE JUST DONE A CHILDISH TRICK [meaning his quick departure]. SIGN BEFORE THEY CHANGE THEIR MINDS." It would be the start of a twenty-eight-year acting career during which he made fifty-five movies. Reagan was at best a decent actor, but he understood his limitations, capitalized on his opportunities, and, as always, had a wonderful sense of timing. In Hollywood, he later recounted, he would transform himself into the character he was portraying and managed to believe whatever he said when he read a script.

He was no prima donna, unlike many of his peers, and became a popular performer in Warner Brothers' "B" pictures, typecast as a handsome and none-too-smart leading man. "Reagan's photographic memory and willingness to take direction were well suited to the assembly-line style of production which Jack Warner had developed," says Reagan biographer Lou Cannon. "The B-picture division of Warner Brothers, a consistent money-maker, turned out films quickly and efficiently, without qualms about artistic quality. An actor who memorized scripts quickly, as Reagan did, was money in the bank. Reagan's easygoing disposition was an additional asset. In the early years he did not agitate for star roles, and he was willing, maybe too willing, to accept a bit role in a big movie after being a hit in a small one. This combination of qualities helped keep Reagan in the second division at Warner's, which was loaded with stars who had Reagan's on-screen wholesomeness but were more difficult to deal with on the set."

His first picture, *Love Is on the Air*, with June Travis, had him conveniently playing a radio announcer. He later admitted that, as a new actor, he came down with "leadingladyitis." He dated his female costar briefly, but nothing came of the relationship. He did eight "B" pictures in eleven months, including *Sergeant Murphy*, which traced the exploits of a horse in the cavalry. He also played a secondary character in a top-level "A" picture, *Submarine D-1*, starring Pat O'Brien, George Brent, and Wayne Morris, but none of his scenes made the final cut. Reagan played yet another radio announcer in *Hollywood Hotel*, an "A" picture starring Dick Powell, who was a major star at the time. Reagan then won a role in *Brother*

Ronald Reagan in Brother Rat, *1938.*

Rat, based on a play about high jinks at a military academy, but rising star Eddie Albert stole the show.

When he wasn't in front of the camera, Reagan became friendly with celebrities such as O'Brien and Powell, as well as James Cagney, Humphrey Bogart, and Frank McHugh. One of the perks of Reagan's contract was that he was allowed to sit at the stars' table at the Warner's studio commissary, joking and talking shop with the big names while they ate lunch. "I was still a Midwest movie fan as far as the gay life of Hollywood was concerned," he explained later. Though he believed at the time that somewhere there was a great swirl of Hollywood parties that he had not yet cracked, Reagan's relatively intimate social circle was, he learned, more the norm. Still, it paid to look in the swing of things. As he relates, "the publicity department saw that I dabbled a bit in café society to secure those candid photographs needed for fan magazine publicity."

This recognition of the need for positive publicity would have huge ramifications. Reagan was learning to be a compliant subject as handlers and public-relations specialists framed his image. Along with the studio's effort to craft him as an average, all-American guy, Reagan benefited from the lucky coincidence of coming from the same town as Louella Parsons, one of Hollywood's most powerful gossip columnists. Sharing roots back in Dixon with the young star gave Parsons a personal, sentimental interest in pushing his career. Not only was she able to promote him on her radio show and in her newspaper column, but she also widened his circle, providing him with access to more of the important names in the movie world.

By 1938 Reagan had moved Jack and Nelle out of Dixon and into a rented apartment in Hollywood and spent his free time with a group of Iowa friends who had come west with him. Pushed by Louella Parsons, his popularity was rising and he was generally liked around the lot, even if some people, like Errol Flynn, found him a bit too goody-goody for their taste. All that was missing was the girl.

Brother Rat changed that.

❖ ❖ ❖

"Where's the rest of me?"

Jane Wyman was born Sarah Jane Fulks in 1914 in St. Joseph, Missouri. She began her movie career in the early thirties as an extra until she finally signed a contract with Warner's in 1936. Both she and Reagan were working up the same ladder of bit parts and "B" films sprinkled with the occasional A film appearance when she took notice of him around the lot. Her marriage was coming apart, and she had filed for divorce when she went on location for the shooting of *Brother Rat*. On the set, Jane finally got to know Reagan better, and soon they were seeing each other regularly, if not exclusively. In 1939 Louella Parsons took a group of actors and actresses on a publicity vaudeville tour called "Hollywood Stars of 1940 on Parade," which included Jane and Dutch. The romance took hold during the trip, and Jane Wyman married Ronald Reagan on January 26, 1940, at the Wee Kirk O'Heather Church in Glendale. Louella Parsons held the reception at her home.

The two had little in common. Reagan liked sports and politics, and she didn't; Wyman enjoyed the nightclub scene, and he did not. Reagan was optimistic by nature, Wyman more of a worrier. Still, they were immediately presented to the world as one of Hollywood's dream couples—all-American boy

"Where is the rest of me?"—*Ronald Reagan's proudest cinematic moment, with Ann Sheridan in* Kings Row, *1942.*

meets all-American girl. Socially they were A-list, with friends such as George Burns, Gracie Allen, and Jack Benny.

Though onscreen usually a demure blonde, Jane was very career-oriented, and her aggressive attitude soon rubbed off on Reagan. One day Reagan read in *Variety* that Warner Brothers was making a movie of Knute Rockne's life, and Pat O'Brien was to play the legendary Notre Dame football coach. With his Midwestern background, Reagan was thoroughly familiar with Rockne's exploits and had earlier told friends that Rockne would be the perfect centerpiece for a movie—with himself playing the legendary Notre Dame running back George Gipp. At Jane's urging he rushed over to see the producer and pleaded for the part, arguing that, like Gipp, he had played football in high school and college. He even produced a few photos of himself in his football uniform at Eureka. His aggressiveness paid off. He won a screen test and got the part.

Reagan called his role "a nearly perfect part from an actor's standpoint. A great entrance, an action middle, and a death scene to finish up." The movie, released by Warner Brothers in 1940, also provided Reagan with a reference point that he would use throughout his political career. After Gipp's tragic death in the film, Rockne motivates his Notre Dame team by asking them to win one for "the Gipper." Reagan would repeat the line whenever he tried to motivate voters for his own campaigns. The fact that Gipp had gambled, smoked, and drank did not seem to matter.

Reagan's performance in *Knute Rockne, All-American* landed him the second lead in *Santa Fe Trail*, starring Errol Flynn. Reagan played a young Lieutenant George Armstrong Custer, and Flynn played J. E. B. Stuart, the Confederate cavalry leader during the Civil War. Dutch now went into his best stretch of film work. Well supported by the studio, Reagan played in *The Badmen*, with Wallace Beery, Lionel Barrymore, and Laraine Day, and *Dark Victory*, with Bette Davis, George Brent, and Humphrey Bogart. Reagan's most celebrated performance was as playboy Drake McHugh in *Kings Row*, released in 1942 and costarring Ann Sheridan. McHugh draws the enmity of his girlfriend's father, who drugs him and amputates his legs while he is unconscious. When McHugh awakes, he realizes the truth and asks, "Where is the rest of me?"—hence the name of Reagan's first autobiography. *Kings Row* featured what Reagan considered the finest acting of his career, and at the time he felt that he was about to break into the top tier.

Reagan summed up his philosophy of acting—and later, of politics and leadership—in his autobiography in 1965.

"So much of our profession is taken up with pretending, with the interpretation of never-never roles, that an actor must spend at least half his waking hours in fantasy, in rehearsal or shooting. If he is only an actor, I feel he is much like I was in *Kings Row*, only half a man—no matter how great his talents. I regard acting with the greatest affection; it has made my life for me. But I realize it tends to become an island of exaggerated importance."

To Reagan, modern living had stripped a good deal of visceral excitement from day-to-day life; without having to hunt for food or worry about becoming another predator's next meal, we are left with only the cathartic power of drama to give us that charge. Reagan wrote, "We've kept a little stardust in our mundane lives by identifying with make-believe characters in make-believe adventures in the house of illusion—the theater. The house lights dim, the curtains part, and for a few hours all women are again beautiful and beloved, all men brave and noble of character. We laugh, cry, know anger, grief, and triumph—then go home at peace with our corner of the world."

Reagan would later extend his concept of drama to politics, with great success. He always felt that, as governor and especially as president, Americans wanted him to keep "a little stardust" in their lives. He made politics-as-theater into an art form—for both good and ill—by creating a White House of illusion.

❖ ❖ ❖

"A near-hopeless hemophilic liberal"

By the end of 1941, the combined incomes of Reagan and Wyman placed them among the well-to-do. The year had seen the birth of their first daughter, Maureen, in January, but also the death of Jack Reagan in May, and though Reagan's most recent films had been of a better sort than he'd been in before, none of them had been the critical or popular success he had hoped for. War and politics hung heavy in the air, and especially so at the Reagan household. Reagan's strong and vocal convictions ran counter to Jane's quiet yet considered distaste for politics, and she was soon getting tired of being ignored at dinner parties while Dutch either got into an argument or gave a speech. Though she was always active in the Screen Actors' Guild (SAG), when she was asked by the union to join the board of directors as an alternate, she put her husband forward, knowing that he was better suited and perhaps hoping that it would channel his political energies.

With the bombing of Pearl Harbor, Reagan could no longer avoid military service. He entered active duty in the army as a second lieutenant on April 19, 1942. He had served as a reserve cavalry officer prior to the war because he enjoyed riding horses. Because of his weak eyesight, he saw no combat but participated in USO tours and other morale-boosting activities for the troops. He was assigned to the Army Air Corps motion-picture unit and worked at various sites in California to make training films, rising to the rank of captain.

It was a stolid and humdrum period of his life, but it began to shape his political perceptions. "I think the first crack in my staunch liberalism appeared in the last year and a half of my military career," he wrote. Despite an army order that every military installation reduce its civilian employees by 35 percent over six months, by the end of the six months the Defense Department had more civilian workers than when the "reduction" started. "If I suggested that an employee might be expendable, his supervisor would look at me as if I were crazy.

Reagan with his wife Jane Wyman and their children, Maureen and Michael, in 1946.

He didn't want to *reduce* the size of his department; his salary was based to a large extent on the number of people he supervised. He wanted to increase it, not decrease it."

The period also produced the first serious cracks in his marriage. Until 1943, Jane Wyman had been consigned to making a string of bad comedies, but then she was given a lead role in *The Lost Weekend*, a role for which she earned an Academy Award nomination. Jane's interest in a career, which had never slackened, was stoked even higher just as she was left alone to raise their daughter. Reagan was able to visit frequently from his post, but he was not an active presence in the home.

After leaving the army in August 1945, Reagan took a few months off. The war years had changed many things. The Reagans had adopted their second child, Michael. Jane's stature was increasing. She took the role as the mother in *The Yearling* for which she was nominated as best actress, while Reagan returned to a growing list of disappointing films at Warner Brothers. The death of FDR and a friendship with conservative SAG president George Murphy, developed in the army, were pushing Reagan away from his Democratic past, and he was now regularly giving speeches in which he railed against the dangers of communism. Murphy secured him a place as a permanent board member of SAG, and the most important changes in Reagan's life began.

As Jane turned more toward her career, Reagan flung himself into SAG and Hollywood politics. Disputes between management and labor and within the union movement itself were plunging Hollywood into one of the most bitter periods in its history. Outside influences were also involved: Communists, gangsters, and union bosses saw the movie business as a profitable opportunity, and they sought to influence or control it as much as possible. Reagan not only found himself in the middle of many controversies that he found fascinating, but he was also serving on the board with some of the biggest celebrities of his day, including Robert Montgomery, Charles Boyer,

James Cagney, Eddie Cantor, Cary Grant, and Dick Powell. These expanding connections provided Reagan with more access to those at the top of the film industry, and added to a growing sense around Hollywood that he was becoming a force to be reckoned with, if not on the screen, then off it.

Because of his role in SAG, Reagan was on the side of the labor unions. He was also deaf to rumors that Communists were infiltrating the entertainment industry in an effort to change America's cultural consciousness. "I knew little and cared less about the rumors about Communists," he wrote. "I was a near-hopeless hemophilic liberal." Though it hardly qualified him as a "fellow traveller," he had always, like his father, voted Democratic, the party of his once and now former hero FDR, and had continued to do so even up to the 1948 election and his vote for Truman.

Though he never liked to admit it, Reagan's idealism led him to join briefly in the mid-forties the Hollywood Independent Committee of the Arts, Sciences, and Professions, which a California legislative committee called in 1947 an important Communist front in California. He also was a member of the liberal American Veterans Committee and the United World Federalists, which supported a global government. He hastily dropped out of both organizations because they seemed too impractical and hazy in their objectives, and he later said all three groups were too left-wing, adding that his associations with them were mistakes. Reagan did campaign, though, for Helen Gahagan Douglas, the liberal Democrat who was demonized by Richard Nixon in the 1950 Senate race in California.

According to some historians, the Communists had two periods of influence in Hollywood. The first was during the Popular Front collaboration of Communists and liberals beginning in 1936 and ending in 1939 with the Nazi-Soviet nonaggression pact; the second period of influence came after Germany invaded the USSR in June 1941 and ended with the Nazi defeat in April 1945, when Stalin ordered Communist parties around the world to stop cooperating with the Western democracies. The Conference of Studio Unions emerged as a force to be reckoned with during the second period, from 1941 to 1945. It tried to exert control over the labor movement in Hollywood and was linked to Communist influences by the House Un-American Activities Committee (HUAC). The Screen Actors' Guild opposed the Conference of Studio Unions' power grab and, despite threats of violence that caused him at one point to carry a gun, Reagan remained steadfast in the guild's struggle.

Within the Screen Actors' Guild, arguments over jurisdiction, wages, and hours only deepened long-held animosities that divided the entertainment-industry unions among themselves, breeding what Reagan considered chaos among painters, machinists, camera operators, set designers, carpenters, and actors. He was upset by feuds over seemingly arcane issues, such as who would control carpentry work on movie sets. Reagan was shocked to see all the squabbling among labor bosses, and found himself immersed in one of the worst strikes ever to hit Hollywood, beginning on September 12, 1946. There was mass picketing at Warner's and MGM, and Reagan was pulled ever deeper into SAG's deliberations and maneuverings.

As the Soviet Union solidified its hold on satellite countries in Eastern and Central Europe and as Communists moved to take over elsewhere, the Cold War prompted even more hysteria at home, and Hollywood was at the center of a maelstrom of suspicion and paranoia. In 1947 HUAC began investigating "Communist infiltration of the motion-picture industry," and eventually ten screenwriters who refused to cooperate with the

◆ HUAC ◆

ADOLPHE MENJOU TESTIFIES BEFORE THE HOUSE UN-AMERICAN COMMITTEE IN 1947.

The House Committee on Un-American Activities (HUAC) was created in 1945. It represented a troubling extension of congressional authority to investigate people and social movements—especially their thoughts, behaviors, and associations. The first congressional investigation of un-American activities, conducted by the Senate Judiciary Committee, began in September 1918 as World War I drew to a close; the goal was to investigate German sympathies in the U.S. business world. In 1919 the mandate was expanded to include Communist sympathizers. In 1930 the House created a Special Committee to Investigate Communist Activities in the United States, which in 1934 became the Special Committee on Un-American Activities, which was made a permanent committee in January 1945.

HUAC's modern mandate stemmed from congressional efforts to probe alleged subversive movements after World War II, when the anti-Communist paranoia in America was at its worst. There were many abuses.

In looking into alleged Communist infiltration of organized labor, witnesses were allowed to testify in secret and make unsubstantiated charges that individuals and groups were supporting Communist activities. The accused often were not given the right of rebuttal. From 1945 to 1950, HUAC reached the zenith—or nadir—of its power. In 1947 its hearings into alleged Communist influence in the movie industry produced sensational coverage in the press as a parade of famous stars, ranging from Robert Montgomery to Ronald Reagan, were quizzed about their political views and the views of others in the film business. Many writers and actors accused of Communist leanings were blacklisted and denied employment for years.

HUAC then moved on to investigating alleged Communist influence in the U.S. government, which resulted in the perjury conviction of State Department official Alger Hiss and brought considerable attention to a young committee member named Richard Nixon. Civil libertarians and liberals accused the committee of abusing witnesses by citing them for contempt when they pleaded their Fifth Amendment right against self-incrimination.

HUAC was renamed the Internal Security Committee in 1969 amid rising criticism that, through intimidation and overzealous pursuit of "subversives," HUAC was undermining free speech and free expression. The committee was abolished by Congress in January 1975, its functions transferred to the House Judiciary Committee.

RONALD REAGAN AT THE HUAC HEARINGS, OCTOBER 1947.

committee went to jail and hundreds of others were kept out of work because they failed to cooperate or were suspected of being Communists or associated with "Reds."

Reagan was elected president of the Screen Actors' Guild in 1947, a post he held until 1952. As historian Garry Wills reports, Reagan and Wyman both gave information to the FBI, something Reagan had done as far back as 1941, but Reagan now took it even further, becoming an informant for the bureau just as he was taking over the presidency of the union, a position that would make him privy to much confidential information. He testified before HUAC and took a conservative but, relative to the times, nonextreme course. He agreed that Communists were trying to subvert the film industry and insert pro-Communist propaganda into American culture. He also voiced the conviction that the movies had tremendous power to shape public opinion, that Communist subversion of Hollywood would have profound consequences if it occurred, and that the Communists had to be stopped from taking over the film industry.

Later, one of his targets in Hollywood was the Committee for the First Amendment, which was active in the 1950s and which Reagan described as a Communist front designed to undermine support for the anti-Communist investigations of HUAC. To his discredit, he defended the blacklist—the refusal by Hollywood producers knowingly to employ Communists or those who refused to answer questions under oath about possible Communist affiliations. Reagan would write in 1990, about this period: "I heard whispers that Moscow wanted to infiltrate the world's most powerful medium of entertainment, but I'd passed them off [at first] as irrational and emotional red baiting. . . . I knew from firsthand experience how Communists used lies, deceit, violence, or any other tactic that suited them to advance the cause of Soviet expansionism. I knew from the experience of hand-to-hand combat that America faced no more insidious or evil threat than that of Communism."

Still, in making his case in public, Reagan showed a milder side that reflected his civil-libertarian streak. He testified that the best way to fight the Communists working in the film industry was not by persecution but through vigorous democratic trade unionism, and to his credit he did not name any alleged Communists or Communist sympathizers before HUAC.

In 1947 he told columnist Hedda Hopper that America should combat communism, or tyranny of any sort, by increasing freedom and improving living conditions for everyone—a decidedly middle-of-the-road view, considering the right-wing tenor of the times. "The Reds know that if we can make America a decent living place for all of our people, their cause is lost here," he said. "So they seek to infiltrate liberal organizations just to smear and discredit them. I've already pulled out of one organization [the Hollywood Independent Committee of the Arts, Sciences, and Professions] that I joined in completely good faith. One day I woke up, looked about, and found it was Commie-dominated. You can't blame a man for aligning himself with an institution he thinks is humanitarian, but you can blame him if he deliberately remains with it after he knows it has fallen into the hands of the Reds."

<><><>

"The Hollywood dream marriage was over."

Reagan's immersion in Hollywood politics was having a disastrous effect where he felt it the most—at home. Reagan and Wyman found their interests were diverging to an extent fatal to their marriage. In June 1947 Wyman gave birth to a baby girl, four months premature, and the infant died the following day. At the time, Reagan was recovering from a life-threatening bout of viral pneumonia caught while making another undistinguished film, leaving Wyman alone while she endured the miscarriage. Each dealt with the pain by becoming immersed in the separate interests they held. Though Wyman did not win the Oscar for *The Yearling*, she was cast as a deaf-mute in the film *Johnny Belinda*, a role to which she applied herself to an almost obsessive depth that matched Reagan's with SAG. Wyman did not share Reagan's shifting beliefs and began to take more than passing interest in her costar from *Johnny Belinda*, Lew Ayres.

When Reagan and Wyman finally divorced in 1948, after eight years, the breakup upset him deeply. Reagan hardly mentions Wyman in his 1965 autobiography beyond saying that he met her in 1939 while making *Brother Rat* and adding that he would never publicly discuss what happened between them. Reagan did not contest the divorce, and Wyman kept custody of the children. The Hollywood dream marriage was over.

As Reagan's political role increased, his career sagged. One reason for his career woes was that the movie business was having economic troubles, partly because of the rise of television, and Reagan was being offered unimportant parts in mediocre movies. One role he did take in 1951, a role indicative of this period in his life, was the chimp-minding college professor in *Bedtime for Bonzo*. In an effort to regain his reputation (at least in his own mind) as a star, he turned down a succession of weak roles and estimated that he gave up $500,000 in film offers; he remained unemployed for fourteen months. Unfortunately, it was a strategy that might have worked earlier in his career, when he was younger and on the rise. As it was, Reagan had reached middle age, and his relationship with Warner Brothers worsened until he finally left the studio in January 1952. At one point he tried a nightclub act in Las Vegas, serving as master of ceremonies for a group called The Continentals; his main responsibility was to introduce the acts and indulge in light banter with comedians, dancers, and other entertainers. It was a serious setback for someone who had been on the cusp of stardom, no matter how optimistic he was.

Ronald Reagan's career as a movie actor was over.

circa 1955

CHAPTER THREE

IDEOLOGUE

Though most movie actors in the fifties had a jaundiced view of television as the last stop before retirement, Reagan's stint in Las Vegas left him with few choices. He agreed in 1954 to host a new dramatic series on television sponsored by General Electric at an annual salary of $125,000. Reagan's job was to introduce each show and act in some of them. Partly because of his genial presence, "General Electric Theater" became extremely popular; it was nineteenth in the national ratings in 1954–55, rose to tenth in 1955–56, and was the third-most-watched program in 1956–57. It became the No. 1 show in its slot at 9 P.M. Sunday nights on CBS. Reagan's career was rejuvenated, and his responsibilities went beyond the screen. He toured the country for ten weeks a year to promote GE and its products and to increase morale among GE employees and executives. It was a substantial commitment of time and energy. Reagan was afraid of air travel at that time after a particularly frightening flight in a blizzard, so he criss-crossed the country by train as he addressed GE audiences, service clubs, and other business groups about the need for traditional values, free enterprise, and patriotism, sometimes giving fourteen speeches or short talks a day. The trips generally revolved around a visit with executives at a company plant, a brief address to workers, and a banquet at night with a civic group such as a chamber of commerce, to which he would give a lengthy speech. He was outgoing and engaged in public, but distant and restrained in private, as if he were conserving himself for his dealings with the wider world, always making sure to build plenty of time for rest and exercise into his schedule. This was a pattern he continued throughout his life. During his eight years as the company's public spokesman, Reagan visited 125 plants, met 250,000 employees, and spoke to innumerable civic groups over lunch and dinner on what he called the "mashed potato circuit."

The constant touring gave Reagan an opportunity not only to make important contacts in the conservative community but also to hone The Speech, the manifesto of conservatism and personal conviction he had developed over his years of growing visibility. Increasingly immersed in the corporate culture that was paying his salary, he preached against the evils of excessive government regulation. He also learned a great deal about how to stir a crowd, how to pace himself, and how to conserve his voice—all valuable skills for the politician he was to become. He was evolving into one of America's premier defenders of big business and was known widely as a passionate believer in the General Electric slogan "Progress Is Our Most Important Product." A joke made the rounds of Hollywood during this period that attested to Reagan's persuasive powers. A man watched him give a testimonial for

General Electric's nuclear submarine program and was deeply impressed. "I really didn't need a submarine," the man remarked to a friend later, "but I've got one now." GE even remodeled the Reagans' house in Pacific Palisades with electric gadgets ranging from the latest table lamps to porch lights and toasters, so his lifestyle could reflect the part he was playing. "It was now his professional duty to be a conspicuous consumer," historian Garry Wills has written. "General Electric early realized that its task was not simply to sell appliances but to create a desire for the kind of life that craves such appliances." And Reagan was to epitomize that life.

For a while, he was the perfect company man. Even though he eloquently praised America's risk-taking business leaders, he rarely took many risks on his own. Still a product of the Depression, he preferred a comfortable, secure world to one in which he took gambles with his career or his financial future. Gradually, as he traveled in conservative, business-saturated circles, The Speech took on more edge, though Reagan, ever the amiable entertainer, kept his appearances enjoyable, filled with jokes and anecdotes.

By the late 1950s he was complaining that America was going astray in fundamental ways, decrying an erosion of honesty, honor, and patriotism. He said the income-tax law was making the people of America dishonest because it took too much money away from hardworking citizens (including himself) and forced many to hide their real income from the government. His anti-Communist message became so strident that even GE became nervous, and the company asked him to pull back into focusing on GE and its products. Though Reagan had consented in the past to limit his criticism of the Tennessee Valley Authority, a major GE client, and otherwise be supportive of their corporate viewpoints, he refused this request. With the more optimistic

THE SPEECH

Through the late 1950s and 1960s, Ronald Reagan became known in Republican and big business circles for The Speech—an eloquent, easy-listening summary of his personal convictions and, more important, a declaration of principles for the conservative movement. It served as the basis for the famous televised address in support of Barry Goldwater in 1964, and the ideas it contained became the cornerstone of the "Reagan revolution" after he became president. Excerpts:

"I am going to talk of controversial things. I make no apology for this. . . . Those who deplore use of the terms 'pink' and 'leftist' are themselves guilty of branding all who oppose their liberalism as right-wing extremists. How long can we afford the luxury of this family fight when we are at war with the most dangerous enemy ever known to man? If we lose that war, and in so doing lose our freedom, it has been said history will record with the greatest astonishment that those who had the most to lose did the least to prevent its happening. The guns are silent in this war, but frontiers fall while those who should be warriors prefer neutrality. . . .

"James Madison said, 'We base all our experiments on the capacity of mankind for self-government.' This idea that government was beholden to the people, that it had no other source of power except the sovereign people, is still the newest, most unique idea in all the long history of man's relation to man. . . . I suggest to you there is no left or right, only an up or down. Up to the maximum of individual freedom consistent with law and order, or down to the antheap of totalitarianism, and regardless of their humanitarian purpose those who would sacrifice freedom for security have, whether they know it or not, chosen this downward path. . . .

"Already the hour is late. Government has laid its hand on health, housing, farming, industry, commerce, education, and to an ever-increasing degree interferes with the people's right to know. Goverment tends to grow, government programs take on weight and momentum as public servants say, always with the best of intentions, 'What greater service we could render if only we had a little more money and a little more power.' But the truth is that outside of its legiti-

RONALD REAGAN WITH CAMPAIGN
SUPPORTERS BEFORE GIVING A
SPEECH AT THE COMMONWEALTH
CLUB IN SAN FRANCISCO, DURING
HIS 1966 BID FOR GOVERNOR OF
CALIFORNIA.

mate function, government does nothing as well or as economically as the private sector of the economy.

"We approach a point of no return when government becomes so huge and entrenched that we fear the consequences of upheaval and just go along with it. . . . If some among you fear taking a stand because you are afraid of reprisals from customers, clients, or even governments, recognize that you are just feeding the crocodile, hoping he'll eat you last.

"If all of this seems like a great deal of trouble, think what's at stake. We are faced with the most evil enemy mankind has known in his long climb from the swamp to the stars. . . . We are being asked to buy our safety from the threat of the Bomb by selling into permanent slavery our fellow human beings enslaved behind the Iron Curtain. To tell them to give up their hope of freedom because we are ready to make a deal with their slavemasters.

"Alexander Hamilton warned us that a nation that can prefer disgrace to danger is prepared for a master and deserves one. . . . Should Moses have told the children of Israel to live in slavery rather than dare the wilderness? Should Christ have refused the cross? Should the patriots at Concord Bridge have refused to fire the shot heard 'round the world? Are we to believe that all the martyrs of history died in vain?"

Kennedy administration gaining popularity in Washington and facing serious competition on TV from "Bonanza," an action/adventure Western broadcast in color against the black-and-white "General Electric Theater," GE decided that he was too controversial, and they parted ways. "General Electric Theater" was taken off the air in September 1962. Reagan would resume his television career by hosting the nonpolitical dramatic series "Death Valley Days" in 1965, but that stint was short-lived. By now, The Speech had become his life.

He was sought out by business groups and conservative organizations that were upset by the vast accumulation of federal power represented by President Lyndon Johnson's Great Society. Such groups cheered Reagan's attacks on Johnson's domestic policies and on LBJ's desire for détente rather than outright military superiority over the Soviet Union. Reagan shared the conservatives' growing fear that communism posed a severe threat inside the United States; he had seen it in Hollywood, and now he saw the evil of collectivism and Marxism-Leninism spreading to other spheres. He considered it his duty to sound the alarm.

His rhetoric became more dramatic. He attacked government-provided medical care for the elderly—eventually enacted as Medicare—as "socialized medicine" and "a foot in the door of a government takeover of all medicine." He condemned the income tax as "this progressive system spawned by Karl Marx and declared by him to be the prime essential of a socialist state." He attacked urban renewal and farm price supports as wrongheaded federal interventions in the marketplace. He supported making Social Security voluntary "so those who can make better provision for themselves are allowed to do so." He favored ending government programs to provide electricity to rural America. He advocated turning over the Tennessee

Valley Authority to private enterprise. And he became a hero in conservative circles.

Reagan had developed a vision of America based on his past and the country's traditions as he understood them. He came to believe totally in the conservative credo of less government, standing up to communism, and freeing what he considered the innate goodness and ambition of the American people.

His obsession with low taxes can be traced to what he considered the exorbitant income-tax rates after World War II, when marginal tax rates in his bracket ranged between 82 percent and 91 percent. He felt those rates unfairly limited his wealth and provided a reverse incentive for productivity. Later he would raise taxes as California governor and make the state tax system more progressive—a necessity, he argued, because his predecessor had left him a large deficit. Yet he supported the principle of lowering taxes and in 1971 would push a tax-limitation amendment that established Reagan as a serious supporter of tax cuts—a cornerstone of his political philosophy. Tax reduction was the fundamental aspect of the national economic policy during his presidency, and the Depression-era Hawley-Smoot Tariff Act, which imposed high tariffs on imports and spurred protectionist retaliation from other countries, had left him a strong free-trader.

As to his military beliefs, he was briefly a pacifist at Eureka College, but had come to support a strong military in the late 1930s and early 1940s, when Germany and Japan threatened the world. From this period onward he argued that military strength deterred aggression and favored spending "whatever is necessary to deter the enemy," even if it meant deficit spending.

Particularly in Southern California, Reagan became extremely popular among "New Right" conservatives, and he fit in perfectly with the hard-right movement then gathering behind Arizona senator Barry Goldwater's campaign for the presidency in 1964. These were conservatives who felt resentful that the "Rockefeller wing" of the Republican Party—liberal, pro-big government politicians on the East Coast symbolized by New York governor Nelson Rockefeller—had betrayed the soul of conservatism. The GOP, in Goldwater's words, should present "a choice," not "an echo" of the Democrats, and Republicans should reaffirm their commitment to states' rights by condemning the concentration of power in Washington. Goldwater argued that America should confront "Reds" aggressively around the world. It was essentially the same message being delivered, albeit with much more appeal, by Ronald Reagan.

In addition to fueling his conservatism, Southern California shaped Reagan in other ways. He did not live in the California that pioneered the cutting-edge popular trends of the sixties, such as free love, drugs, experimental lifestyles, and environmentalism. Instead, Reagan's economic well-being and connections had made him part of an older California of wealth and convention.

"It is the post-World War II California, represented by a home and a fenced backyard where a family could retreat from the dirt and noise of the city," wrote Reagan biographer Bill Boyarsky. "Most who achieved that dream did so modestly, in tract homes built in flat, unstylish suburbs. The Reagans and their friends were more successful. Their backyards were bigger, their vacation retreats more exclusive, their friends more powerful. But in his view of the world, and in his choice of pastimes, Reagan is the ultimate suburbanite, happiest when he has a fence to build or a tree to plant."

This milieu encouraged his natural tendency to simplify. Life had worked out well for him, so why wouldn't it work out well for everyone? Among his friends and associates in suburban California, his free-market optimism blossomed like a wildflower after a desert thunderstorm.

❧ ❧ ❧

"I. T. W. W. W."

It was during the 1950s and early 1960s that Reagan also forged the partnership that was essential to his political success—his marriage to Nancy Davis.

Four years after the divorce from Jane Wyman, and after an unhappy period of bachelorhood, he married another actress. Nancy Davis had initially contacted him because he was an activist in the Screen Actors' Guild, and she was upset because her name kept appearing on lists of Communist front organizations. Friends, however, suggest that she simply used that story as a pretext to meet a handsome actor whom she had admired from afar. As recounted in his autobiography, they arranged a dinner, got along well, and during the next few months fell in love. They married on March 4, 1952, with actor William Holden as best man and his wife, Ardis Holden, as matron of honor.

Nancy became not only a doting wife who happily gave up her marginal film career for her husband but also Ronald Reagan's best friend and political partner whose importance in his life would grow over time. They had two children—Patti, born prematurely by cesarean section on October 22, 1952, seven and a half months after their marriage, and Ronald Prescott Reagan, born on May 28, 1958.

She was born Anne Frances Robbins in Manhattan in 1921, the same year her father, a car salesman, left the family. Her

Ronald Reagan married Nancy Davis on March 4, 1952.

mother, stage actress Edith Luckett, was away for long periods while traveling for her stage career, and Nancy experienced a lonely early childhood. But when Edith Luckett married Chicago neurosurgeon Loyal Davis, everything changed.

Nancy was seven years old at the time, and, to her delight, her mother quit the theater, moved to Chicago, and began to spend much more time with her daughter. Nancy attended Girls' Latin School, majored in drama at Smith College, and lived a pampered life. Taking a cue from her mother, she made acting her career, performing onstage and then enjoying some success in Hollywood.

Nancy Davis made eleven movies from 1949 to 1957, including *East Side, West Side* with James Mason and Van Heflin and *The Doctor and the Girl* with Glenn Ford, both in 1949; *Night into Morning* with Ray Milland in 1951; and *It's a Big Country* with Fredric March in 1952. She was often typecast as a young wife, pregnant and doting on her man. What she herself yearned for was a traditional family and, since Ronald Reagan wanted the same thing, they were an ideal match.

Mrs. Reagan recalled in her autobiography that her mother taught her how to be a traditional wife. "She cared for her husband, she expanded his social circle—she helped him in every possible way," Mrs. Reagan wrote. " 'Now, Nancy,' she used to say, 'when you get married, be sure to get up and have breakfast with your husband in the morning. Because if you don't, you can be sure that some other woman who lives around the corner will be perfectly happy to do so.' "

Nancy took this advice to heart. "My life didn't really begin until I met Ronnie," she said on many occasions. She called him "Ronnie" and he called her "Mommy," though after he became president he began calling her the more dignified "Nancy," at least in the presence of others.

From their earliest days through the eight years he served as California governor and their eight years in the White House, the schedule remained the same. Reagan would leave work at

5 or 6 P.M. and spend quiet evenings at home with Nancy (and their children, when the kids were young). They would eat a simple dinner such as macaroni and cheese or meat loaf and mashed potatoes, then watch television. Reagan always liked lighter fare, such as "Mission: Impossible" and the Dean Martin show in the 1960s and superficial dramas such as "Dynasty" and "Dallas" in the 1980s.

From the start, Nancy was extremely protective of her husband. She would guard his schedule zealously and insist that he get plenty of rest and have time for leisure activities, such as riding horses. And while she rarely got involved in policy decisions, she tried to undermine aides she felt were not serving her husband well, a pattern she continued with a vengeance in the White House. She could barely tolerate reporters, whom she regarded as prying, ill-mannered ruffians who were always attempting to embarrass her husband. Although that may at times have been true, her curtness and obvious love of wealth and privilege caused the media to portray her as selfish, brittle, and aristocratic. This image would persist and grow in the White House. But without the zone of comfort and support created by Nancy in the 1950s and sustained through their life together, Ronald Reagan could never have achieved what he did. Perhaps more than anything else, she assigned herself the role of making sure he was protected from himself, that his innate goodwill was not exploited. To her, his optimism was a precious commodity, one to be nurtured even if she occasionally got upset because he was being unrealistic. She compared her husband to his mother, Nelle, who believed that people were fundamentally moral and decent. "Nelle never saw anything evil in another human being," Nancy once wrote, "and Ronnie is the same way. Sometimes it infuriates me, but that's how he is. . . . Nelle used to tell her boys that everything happens for a reason, that they might not understand the reason at the time, but eventually they would. Ronnie still believes that." Nancy worried for both of them, got angry for both of them, was suspicious for both of them.

The Reagans in the backyard of their Pacific Palisades, California, home in the 1950s.

Ronald Reagan, with wife Nancy and son Michael, takes the oath of office for governor of California, January 1967.

Reagan returned her affection in many ways. He was never shy about hugging or kissing her in public, holding hands, or expressing his love for her. He would say that coming home to Nancy was like coming out of the cold into a warm room with a fireplace. If she was leaving on a trip, he would put her vitamin pills in a bottle and leave it out for her. He enjoyed leaving her love notes and cards for her birthday, their anniversary, and Valentine's Day, often with a scrawl at the bottom "I.T.W.W.W." for "I love you more than anything In The Whole Wide World."

Reagan's political transformation became complete in personal terms when he formally switched his registration from Democrat to Republican in 1962. His message was now set in stone: Attack centralized government. "This superstructure of government imposed on our original form is composed of bureaus and departments and is unchanged by any election," he told the Executive Club of Chicago in May 1958. "This hierarchy threatens to reverse the relationship of citizen and civil servant."

He emerged as a national figure when he gave a dramatic speech on television for Arizona senator Barry Goldwater, the Republican presidential nominee, on October 27, 1964. Goldwater lost the election in a catastrophic defeat at the hands of Democratic incumbent Lyndon Johnson. But America's conservatives had found a new hero, and eventually they began calling Ronald Reagan "The Great Communicator." A group of ultra-wealthy Californians began grooming him for bigger things, and by 1966 he was running for governor of the Golden State.

February 1972

CHAPTER FOUR

POLITICIAN

A week after Reagan's speech, Goldwater suffered a huge defeat at the hands of Democratic president Lyndon Johnson, and Reagan was the new darling of the American right. Within months, "Friends of Ronald Reagan" had been formed in Los Angeles to lay the groundwork for a Reagan campaign for governor of California.

Goldwater had been easy to caricature as an extremist. Reagan, on the other hand, was self-deprecating and reassuring, even though he was advocating the same creed: less government, lower taxes, cuts in federal programs such as welfare and the popular Social Security entitlement, and standing up to communism. When California elected ex-actor George Murphy, a Reagan pal from his Hollywood days, to the Senate in 1964, Reagan thought it was a good omen. Yet Reagan, while an enthusiastic advocate of conservative causes, was a reluctant candidate.

His millionaire backers would not take maybe for an

answer. Their leader was Holmes Tuttle, owner of several car dealerships and other businesses in the Los Angeles area. Tuttle, a GOP fund-raiser since Dwight Eisenhower was elected president in 1952, was the prime mover in recruiting Reagan to run for governor, and eventually he succeeded.

As the 1966 campaign began, Reagan became the issue. Many Democrats thought he was too extreme and not very smart. He played into their hands by declaring that he would have voted against the Civil Rights Act of 1964, and revealed in his just-published autobiography, *Where's the Rest of Me?*, that he had joined Communist front organizations years earlier but left them when he belatedly realized what they were—making him look like a dupe.

Stuart Spencer and Bill Roberts, his political consultants, hired Behavior Sciences Corporation of Reseda, California, to coach the fifty-five-year-old Reagan on issues. They presented him with eight books of five-by-eight cards containing simple replies to questions likely to come up about California, trying to tailor the replies to his basic message—that an unfettered private sector would improve the economy and enhance society better than government activism. Spencer and Roberts assigned a handler to Reagan at all public appearances, someone to give him last-minute advice on issues, remind him what he was supposed to be saying, and help him avoid gaffes. The handlers realized that Reagan needed rest to perform well, and they scheduled a nap for him frequently in the afternoons. They also used simple TV ads featuring him speaking into a camera—a technique he used with considerable deftness for Goldwater and on "General Electric Theater" and "Death Valley Days."

"He took it all with equanimity, and not only because he was a political novice," historian Garry Wills has observed. "He would continue to take such handling through his political life. . . . Reagan is not, like most of us, plagued by the little vanities—by jokes about his age, or his being an actor, or the statistics he misquotes. His larger confidence in his capacity is unshakable, because not entirely dependent on his own achievements. He really does believe in the ordinary good person of his background, who can preserve values that are more important than expertise."

Democratic governor Pat Brown was one of those who mistakenly dismissed Reagan as a political lightweight who would crumble under pressure. Brown also underestimated the growing conservatism in California and Reagan's ability to exploit it.

The contrast between the two rivals was dramatic: Reagan, a trim, handsome, self-styled "citizen-politician," versus Brown, a rotund, balding, career politician who often looked harsh on television. Making the contrast worse for Brown was his willingness to play hardball, which conveyed the impression of mean-spiritedness when matched against Reagan's easygoing geniality. Brown had been a public figure in California for a generation and had built his liberal reputation on spending vast sums of money on public works projects such as freeways, water projects, and parks, and making huge investments in the state's higher-education system. But his go-along, get-along style made him ripe for defeat, as did the middle class's desire for a respite from high taxes and costly social programs.

When the Watts section of Los Angeles burst into riots in 1965 and into near-riots in 1966, Brown's slow reaction added to public perceptions that he was indecisive and out of touch. These experiences reminded voters of Brown's passive attitude toward student demonstrations at the University of California at Berkeley starting on September 29, 1964, when protesters took over the administration building and began massive sit-ins. Even the governor's fellow party members were not happy with him; Brown was criticized by Democratic Assembly Speaker Jesse Unruh as "the tower of Jell-O."

Using a technique that would bring him the presidency in 1980, Reagan hammered away at Brown for "failed leadership" and wove many subthemes into this overall message—high taxes, the unfairness and cost of welfare, the troubles at the university. Reagan was particularly certain that student protest was upsetting many voters; he was asked about it everywhere he went. His answer was that the students should "observe the rules or get out." Middle-class and working-class voters loved it. Reagan demonstrated a remarkable ability—invaluable to a candidate—to say the same thing over and over with the same freshness, verve, and sincerity as if it were the first time.

Brown, in the end, became desperate and seemed willing to say almost anything to win reelection. At one point he told a group of schoolchildren, "I'm running against an actor, and you know who shot Lincoln, don't ya?" The Republicans ran that simpleminded quote in a barrage of thirty-second and sixty-second ads depicting Brown as a demagogue.

Reagan was elected governor by the extraordinary margin of nearly 1 million votes—winning 3,742,913 votes to Brown's 2,749,174. It was a personal triumph.

❧   ❧   ❧

"I could take some coaching from the sidelines . . ."

When Reagan arrived in Sacramento, he had little idea what he would do, since he knew nothing about government. He had objectives but didn't know how to go about achieving them. Billing himself as a citizen-politician had immense appeal on the campaign trail, but it caused severe problems for Reagan when he took office. In his mind, he didn't need to worry about the details of state problems because his overall principles and good intentions should be enough. They weren't. At a press conference on March 14, 1967, nearly three months after he took office, he was asked to describe his legislative program and drew a blank. "I could take some coaching from the sidelines," he said, looking at his aides for help, "if anyone can recall my legislative program."

Developing a pattern he would use in the White House, he acknowledged the need to compensate for his own limitations and displayed a talent for recruiting loyal staffers who learned

Ronald Reagan alongside wife Nancy, at his inauguration as the 33rd Governor of the State of California, January 5, 1967.

THE KITCHEN CABINET

Holmes Tuttle was the leader of Ronald Reagan's kitchen cabinet of California millionaires who bankrolled his political career.

Tuttle, a longtime Republican fund-raiser who owned several Los Angeles–area car dealerships and other businesses, had known Reagan since he sold him a car in 1946. In 1964 Tuttle organized a $1,000-a-plate dinner in Los Angeles and arranged for Reagan to be the keynote speaker. He was a huge success, and when the speech was broadcast across California, it raised even more money for the GOP. Reagan gave another smashing performance in a televised speech for Republican presidential nominee Barry Goldwater on October 27, 1964, and Tuttle was again impressed.

In January 1965, just after Goldwater suffered a humiliating defeat, Tuttle convened a conference of like-minded, self-made millionaires at his house to talk about running someone against Democratic governor Pat Brown the following year. They decided on Reagan.

"Reagan is the man who can enunciate our principles to the people," said A. C. (Cy) Rubel, board chairman of Union Oil Company. Added Henry Salvatori, founder of Western Geophysical Company:

"Reagan doesn't have great depth, but I don't know any politician who does. He's not the most intelligent man who ever was, but I've never met a politician with great depth."

Tuttle and most of his associates were elderly or middle-aged entrepreneurs who had come to California from the Midwest in the 1930s and had amassed huge fortunes. And they wanted Reagan to return California as much as possible to a laissez-faire economy. "We believed in the free enterprise system," Tuttle explained. "We felt that if it was going to be preserved, instead of going around belly-aching about it we should go out and do something about it."

Tuttle met with Reagan, who expressed strong doubts about running. Tuttle pushed the issue by meeting with Stuart Spencer and Bill Roberts, two political consultants and managers from Southern California who had run former New York governor Nelson Rockefeller's impressive (but unsuccessful) presidential primary campaign there in 1964. "We checked with people around the country, and they said Spencer-Roberts was the best," Tuttle recalled. "We didn't want anything less than the best."

Spencer-Roberts agreed to manage a Reagan campaign if the actor decided to run. Tuttle presented

Reagan with the ready-made political team, and Reagan finally agreed to be the candidate.

By the spring of 1965, "Friends of Ronald Reagan" had blossomed into a group of forty-one wealthy donors who ensured that his gubernatorial campaign would never be strapped for cash. After he won the election in November 1966, Lyn Nofziger, a key aide to the governor-elect, said, "Ronald Reagan materialized out of thin air with no political background, no political cronies, and no political machine. . . . He didn't even run his own campaign. His campaign was run by hired people who then walked away and left it. Therefore, when he was elected, the big question was, 'My God, what do we do now?' "

Tuttle and his millionaires had plenty of ideas, especially on filling personnel slots. They formed the "Major Appointments Task Force" and helped Reagan choose lawyers William French Smith, Caspar Weinberger, William Clark, and Ed Meese for his administration, all of whom would follow him to Washington when he would become president fourteen years later. They remained close advisers during his governorship, pressing him to lessen government regulations as much as possible, which he endeavored to do.

The kitchen cabinet also helped Reagan get elected president, provid-

GOVERNOR REAGAN SIGNS A DEATH PENALTY BILL.

ing him with start-up contributions and counsel. At this point the millionaires' group included Tuttle, Salvatori, Smith, publisher Walter Annenberg, Colorado beer producer Joseph Coors, drugstore magnate Justin Dart, steel millionaire Earle Jorgensen, and real-estate tycoon William Wilson.

As Reagan prepared to take over the federal government in late 1980, they set up shop in Washington and guided Reagan as he filled his cabinet and other senior policy-making jobs with multimillionaires and hard-line conservatives, including two members of the kitchen cabinet itself—Smith as attorney general and Charles Wick as director of the U.S. Information Agency.

After Reagan settled into office, the kitchen cabinet faded in importance, but Ronald and Nancy Reagan continued to socialize with them and considered them close friends.

fast, and he delegated great amounts of power to them. Reagan turned over the day-to-day operation of the governor's office to Philip Battaglia, a brilliant thirty-two-year-old Pasadena lawyer who had served as Reagan's campaign manager and was named the new governor's executive secretary. Lyn Nofziger was communications director. Tuttle and other wealthy businessmen exerted power as members of Reagan's kitchen cabinet. Also influential were William French Smith, Reagan's lawyer; William Clark, his cabinet secretary; and Taft Schreiber, an MCA executive and informal adviser.

Clark would develop one-page "minimemos" that reduced complex issues to four paragraphs: one to state the problem, one to present the facts, a third for discussion, and a final paragraph to recommend courses of action. The memo system typified Reagan's approach to governing: simplistic, efficient, and unencumbered by details.

Reagan's popularity grew as his policies began to take effect. At first he proposed cutting each department's spending by 10 percent but found he was penalizing efficient departments along with inefficient ones, so he backed off. On March 28, Smith presented the legislature with a new Reagan budget totaling $5.06 billion, an increase of $440 million. To the chagrin of conservatives, it was California's first $5 billion budget. Reagan, however, scored points with conservative voters when he was able to cut the budget for the costly and unpopular Department of Mental Hygiene, which ran the state's mental hospitals (even though he had refused to visit any of the hospitals to see conditions firsthand, including the effects of staff shortages).

On June 13, 1967, Reagan signed a bill liberalizing abortion in California by allowing the procedure in cases of rape or incest, or if a doctor found that continuing a pregnancy would endanger the life or health of the mother. Francis Cardinal McIntyre, a prominent Roman Catholic prelate, warned Reagan that this latter provision would permit many abortions, but Reagan went along with the bill's GOP sponsors and medical authorities who insisted that doctors would not overdo the procedure.

Reagan agonized over this decision more than virtually any other that he dealt with as governor. The bill Reagan signed in effect allowed abortion on demand, and he later came to abhor it. He blamed the vast proliferation of abortions on doctors' and psychiatrists' taking advantage of a "loophole" that he was unaware of when he signed the legislation, but this was a distortion; he was told, by McIntyre and others, exactly what would happen. He considered this abortion bill one of the worst mistakes of his political career, but it crystallized his thinking. From then on, he would argue that abortion was murder and could only be justified in self-defense—if the mother's life were in danger. And he would later advocate the Human Life Amendment that would impose a constitutional ban on abortion.

Yet on other social issues, Reagan was far from a conservative crusader. He believed that homosexuality was a sickness—this belief a remnant of his boyhood in Dixon—but he had learned in Hollywood to tolerate unorthodox lifestyles and behaviors. Despite the urging of some of his conservative supporters, he never made fighting homosexuality a cause. In the final analysis, Reagan felt that what people do in private is their own business, not government's.

Reagan's stewardship over the environment also was more middle-of-the-road than his critics had feared. He had complained about how government's environmental regulations were hindering private enterprise. And he had made some foolish statements about environmental issues, including the comment, "A tree is a tree—how many more do you need to look at?" But his record turned out to be surprisingly moderate.

During his administration, two state agencies were created to control waste and air pollution and to help regulate nuclear power plant sites—a strengthening of government's hand. He agreed to create Redwood National Park. He halted construction of a dam that would have flooded the scenic Round Valley in northern California and forced the uprooting of Native Americans who lived there. In this case, he stood up to land developers and powerful farmers and sided with conservationists. He backed bond issues to expand park land and upgrade water quality.

The reason he modified his views was because a key aide—Norman (Ike) Livermore, secretary of the state resources agency—was an environmentalist who knew the details of environmental issues far better than the governor did and pushed aggressively to have his views implemented. In addition, Reagan succumbed to pressure from the state legislature and the growing California environmental movement to preserve the state's natural resources.

Yet at heart, Reagan preferred to leave environmental issues to local government if at all possible. In 1972 he said "state government should intercede in local matters only where necessary" and noted that "the protection of environmental resources of statewide significance is principally a local government responsibility." In the late 1970s Reagan would strongly support the "Sagebrush Rebellion" in which powerful farmers, ranchers, developers, and political figures in the West agitated for the transfer of huge tracts of federal land to states and private interests. By that point, economic hard times had forced the environmental movement into retreat, and Reagan's natural impulses to cut the role of government overcame the moderation he had displayed during his years as governor.

His record on the environment showed that, far from being

an insensitive right-wing ideologue, he was a clever politician who knew how to adjust to the political winds.

❧ ❧ ❧

"Ladies and gentlemen, if there are any—"

The area in which Reagan achieved notoriety as a hard-line conservative was in standing up to student protesters. This made him a villain for many, but a hero to working-class and middle-class traditionalists. His running battle with the University of California was one of his most bitter struggles.

Only a few weeks after his inauguration, he became embroiled in a confrontation with students and faculty members. They were seething at the new governor's proposals to cut the education budget by 10 percent and impose for the first time a tuition of $400 a year at the university and $200 a year at state colleges.

On February 11, 1967, an angry group of demonstrators organized by the American Federation of Teachers, some bearded and carrying signs saying "Tax the Rich," marched on the state capitol in Sacramento. Reagan immediately realized the political value in confronting them, and overruled the advice of aides who wanted him to rush out of town for a previously scheduled speech in Portland, Oregon. Instead, Reagan surprised the protesters by showing up to chat. He was greeted with boos and derision.

"Ladies and gentlemen, if there are any—" Reagan began. More boos.

"The people do have some right to have a voice in the principles and basic philosophy that will go along with the education they provide," Reagan shouted over the tumult. "As governor, I am going to represent the people of the state."

The protesters shouted him down and began chanting, "We are people."

Reagan, unable to continue, left the scene but made sure to stop long enough to give his reaction to reporters at the Capitol rotunda. Looking firm and unruffled, he declared, "If they represent the majority of the student body of California, then God help the university and the college system."

That is exactly the way most California voters felt about student radicals, and Reagan's performance, carried on television and in the newspapers, was a big hit. He knew that many of his constituents were fed up with what they considered permissiveness, boorish behavior, and irresponsibility on campus, especially at Berkeley, which was becoming synonymous with student radicalism. They wanted their governor to remain reasonable but to stand up to the campus extremists in no uncertain terms, just as Reagan had done.

At one point in February 1969, students trying to attend classes at Berkeley were roughed up by protesters who said they represented the "Third World Liberation Front." Reagan declared a state of emergency and sent in the California Highway Patrol to protect the school from "criminal anarchists" and "off-campus revolutionaries." The situation deteriorated, as riots and firebombings shook both Berkeley and the surrounding community. By May, radicals and others had occupied university-owned land, declaring it a "people's park," and stoned police. A riot resulted, and one young man was killed by a shotgun blast fired by a law officer. Many were injured and arrested. Reagan sent in the National Guard for seventeen days and later argued that his action had prevented further deaths and restored order.

As governor, Reagan's relationship with student movements was often stormy.

Such hard-line positions were making Reagan even more of a darling to conservatives across the country. By mid-1967, after only a few months in office, some Reagan advisers, including political and media strategist Lyn Nofziger and oil millionaire Tom Reed, were urging him to run for president. They argued that the leading contenders were all lacking— Nelson Rockefeller of New York and George Romney of Michigan were too moderate, and Richard Nixon had the reputation of a loser, and a sore loser at that. Reagan allowed his supporters to take soundings and do some preliminary planning on his behalf but never authorized a full-fledged campaign. He told friends he thought the whole effort was premature, since he had been governor for less than a year. His backers, however, persuaded him not to make any irrevocable decisions about staying out of the 1968 race.

By early 1968 the quasi-campaign was rendered moot when Nixon ran up a string of primary victories and locked up the GOP nomination. Yet Reagan had been bitten by presidential ambition. He received an enthusiastic reception during a speaking tour of the South that summer, and he received further encouragement from members of the California delegation to the Republican National Convention, which he headed as favorite son.

Reagan's judgment was clouded by his popularity among conservatives and his aides' enthusiasm. He believed that Nixon's support was soft, especially in southern delegations. And he was pushed into action when former California senator Bill Knowland advised him just before the convention opened in Miami Beach that Ohio governor James Rhodes, also a favorite-son candidate, was trying to deny Nixon a first-ballot victory. Knowland said that if Reagan declared himself an active candidate at the last moment, it would open the floodgates of doubt about Nixon and could derail his nomination. Reagan accepted the scenario and declared himself an active candidate as the convention began, a rash move that, in the end, embarrassed him considerably because he generated virtually no delegate support outside California. Nixon was nominated overwhelmingly and went on to defeat Democratic nominee Hubert Humphrey in the general election. But Reagan had tasted presidential politics and liked it. He had impressed many GOP activists, and they would not forget him.

Moving to Sacramento forced Nancy Reagan to make adjustments as well. The first was to move out of the Governor's Mansion. Situated on a busy intersection, abutting an American Legion hall, the building was a Victorian pile in great need of repair. When first shown the house, Nancy remained politely quiet, but after four months amid its tattered decoration, noise, drafts, and regular fire alarms, she could take it no longer: The state's First Family rented a home in the suburbs. The Reagans' wealthy friends happily donated furnishings—all tax-deductible—and later went so far as to band together and buy the entire house for $150,000, then lease it back to the Reagans for the same $1,250 a month they had paid originally.

The move was hardly a public relations success for Reagan, but as he learned his way around the governor's office, Nancy's perceived arrogance and wealthy tastes deflected some criticism from him. An interview with writer Joan Didion that appeared in *The Saturday Evening Post* especially infuriated her. While Nancy felt that she had been extremely friendly and forthcoming with the reporter, Didion drew a portrait of a woman whose daily routine seemed more like a movie role than an actual life. If Nancy had been leery of the press before, she was now blatantly distrustful. Still, she continued to shop at designer boutiques and get back to Beverly Hills as often as possible.

Over time, family problems also complicated the Reagans' home life. Maureen was working in public relations for an airline, and Michael was racing boats and looking for sponsors. Ostensibly because of the possibility of conflict of interest, they were kept away from their father. Patti developed into a collegiate leftist—not unusual considering the times, but of great concern to the Reagans—and Ron, Jr., was high-spirited, though sometimes the target of classmates. As hard as Nancy tried, it was sometimes difficult to maintain the facade of a happy family.

❖ ❖ ❖

"We simply cannot sit idly by and do nothing . . ."

By 1970, the last year of his first term, Reagan had achieved only modest changes with his conservative agenda, and he was eager to find an issue on which he could campaign as the centerpiece of his second term. He decided that welfare reform would fill, the bill, and he campaigned aggressively with a promise to overhaul the costly and unpopular system, which he called "the greatest domestic problem facing the nation today and the reason for the high cost of government."

His reelection bid got a big boost when the Democrats nominated former Assembly Speaker Jesse Unruh, long a political power broker in Sacramento and known in the press and among his critics as "Big Daddy." Unruh portrayed Reagan as a puppet of millionaires. For his part, Reagan portrayed Unruh as a power-hungry bully and a demagogue, and billed himself as a citizen-politician trying to clean up the mess left by Unruh and other professional politicians, even though at this point Reagan had been governor for nearly four years.

As in 1966 (and again in the 1980 and 1984 presidential campaigns), Reagan benefited from the contrast with his rival. Unruh's biography contained elements of a success story similar to Reagan's: Unruh came from a poor family that had migrated through Kansas and Texas; he moved to California in 1940 and overcame a lisp to attend college; he worked at odd jobs and was elected to the State Assembly at age thirty-two. In 1961 he was elected Speaker of the Assembly at age thirty-nine.

But Unruh was a man of large appetites, a hard drinker and fancy dresser who at one point weighed more than 280 pounds (although he slimmed down to 200 for his campaign against Reagan). He had a tendency to lose his temper when he suffered a legislative setback, and he often bullied his colleagues. Unruh also had close ties to lobbyists. While he eventually endorsed political reforms, such as providing legislators with a top-notch research and staffing operation so they would not have to rely on lobbyists for information, he reveled in the perquisites of power. Although he was eleven years younger than Reagan, Unruh became closely identified with old-style wheeling and dealing. In the end, he suffered from the phrase he had proudly used in the legislature: "Money is the mother's milk of politics."

The citizen-politician theme proved popular (as it would when Reagan ran for president in 1976 and 1980). Reagan won a second term in 1970 with more than 3.4 million votes, or 52.9 percent of the total, to Unruh's 2.9 million votes or 45.1 percent. Even more remarkable, Reagan survived despite major setbacks for the Republicans and the Nixon administration nationally. The GOP lost nine seats in the House of Representatives (while gaining two in the Senate) and lost eleven governorships. In California, Democrat John Tunney defeated Republican senator George Murphy, Reagan's pal from Hollywood, and Democrats gained three seats in the California Assembly and two in the state Senate, taking control of both houses of the legislature.

Faced with opposition control in the legislature, Reagan was forced to become more focused in his second term. As he had promised, he zeroed in on welfare reform as his top priority.

Reagan was increasingly alarmed about the soaring increase in welfare recipients receiving assistance under the Aid to Families with Dependent Children (AFDC) program. In California alone, the AFDC caseload had gone up from 375,000 recipients in 1963 to 769,000 in 1967, Reagan's first year in office, to 1,566,000 at the end of 1970. Reagan began referring to welfare as a "monster," and he promised to tame it.

While the federal government had created AFDC in 1935 and still paid part of the costs, the states set the level of benefits. There had been no increase in those benefits in

California since 1957, as both Governors Pat Brown, a Democrat, and Reagan, a Republican, had frozen the allotments to save the taxpayers money. But from a budgetary standpoint the real problem was not the level of benefits to individual recipients but the fact that the number of recipients was soaring.

Reagan proposed to severely limit eligibility in his California Welfare Reform Act of 1971. His goals, included in seventy specific proposals, were to increase aid to the truly needy; require the able-bodied to work, seek employment, or get training; equalize health benefits so those receiving government-financed care got service similar to that received by those covered by private insurance; and "strengthen family responsibility as the basic element in our society." It was a commonsense but tough-minded approach that many other states would eventually emulate.

Reagan got personally involved in the campaign to sell his ideas and invested more of himself in welfare reform than in any other issue. "We simply cannot sit idly by and do nothing to prevent an uncontrolled upward spiraling of the welfare caseload, as most other states and the federal government appear resigned to do," Reagan asserted in unveiling his recommendations. "The whole system itself is about to collapse, nationwide, from the burden it is placing on the taxpayer each year. . . . Additionally, the system does not adequately provide for the truly needy. Virtually everywhere in California the truly needy are barely subsisting, many below the poverty line, while thousands of the less needy with other sources of income and various exemptions and disregards are getting a disproportionate share of the available money."

Working with the Democratic majority in the legislature, he eventually won passage of welfare reform, and it became one of the success stories of his tenure in Sacramento. Within three years the AFDC caseload had dropped from 1,608,000 to 1,330,000, and Reagan had an important addition to his presidential portfolio.

Reagan also showed that he was not a draconian right-winger on tax policy and social issues; instead, he was a mainstream conservative. He agreed to the withholding of state income tax, which he had opposed during his first four years. And he agreed with the Democratic legislature on a plan to increase the sales tax by one cent; this revenue was combined with federal revenue-sharing programs and a state surplus to finance a politically canny $1 billion in property-tax relief as well as a more equitable financing system for public schools. During his eight years, Reagan increased spending by 89 percent for elementary and secondary schools, compared with 71 percent during Pat Brown's eight years.

Under Reagan, the state budget went up from $4.6 billion a year to $10.2 billion—more than double. But Reagan also did much to control government growth, especially in the state workforce. The number of state employees grew by only half the rate of growth during the Brown years. (In the process, it turned out that Reagan had paid no state taxes in 1970; he said some of his investments had gone bad. He suffered some embarrassment over the revelation, but nothing that severely damaged his popularity over the long term.)

Reagan also signed more than forty bills increasing sentences for criminals and making other changes in the criminal justice system. Such steps were popular, even though crime did not decline greatly.

It was a solid if not spectacular record, but it was enough to propel him to the next level in politics.

Reagan did not seek reelection as governor in 1974 and almost immediately set about running for president in 1976.

❖ ❖ ❖

"We bought it, we paid for it, it's ours, and we're going to keep it."

It was not an easy time to be a Republican because of the growing Watergate scandal, but Reagan never lost faith. In a remarkable display of loyalty and naïveté, he defended President Richard Nixon and his party almost to the last.

On February 12, 1974, Reagan, ever the optimist, sounded a call to arms at a Lincoln Day dinner for Republicans in Oklahoma City. Arguing that the GOP needed to take on its critics, he said, "We in our party have too often been the victims of big-city political machines voting tombstones, warehouses, and empty lots against us in every election." Finally, on August 6, 1974, after all the pro-Nixon Republicans on the House Judiciary Committee had abandoned their president over Watergate, Reagan saw the light. He admitted that "neither the Congress nor the American people had been told the entire truth about Watergate." Nixon resigned a few days later. President Gerald Ford's pardon of Nixon in September added to public outrage against the Republicans, and the GOP lost forty-three seats in the House, four in the Senate, and four governorships, including California's, in November 1974.

Yet Reagan left the governorship in January 1975 as a popular GOP leader despite his party's woes. Under the guidance of Washington lawyer and former Nixon political adviser John Sears, Reagan began planning for 1976. Since Ford had succeeded to the Oval Office after Nixon's resignation, such a run would involve challenging an incumbent Republican president, a daunting task. But Reagan and other conservative leaders were angered when Ford named liberal New York governor Nelson Rockefeller as his vice president, raising questions about whether Ford would sell out the principles of the right to appeal to a wider constituency. Ford would let Rockefeller drop off the GOP ticket in 1976, but by then Reagan's unofficial presidential campaign was going strong.

For his part, Reagan was disappointed and increasingly upset with Ford, and not only because of the Rockefeller appointment as vice president (which Reagan wanted for himself). Reagan was upset with Ford for proposing limited amnesty for Vietnam War draft evaders and deserters, and he felt that the incumbent was not conservative enough across the board. When Ford offered Reagan a possible ambassadorship to the Court of St. James's or an appointment as secretary of transportation, Reagan turned him down.

As he preserved his option of challenging Ford in 1976, Reagan returned to "the mashed potato circuit" and spent 1975 making up to 10 speeches a month at an average fee of $5,000 per speech. He took many of his ideas and statistics from *Reader's Digest* and *Human Events*, a conservative journal, and wrote a column that appeared in 174 newspapers. His commentaries also were broadcast on more than 200 radio stations. Biographer Lou Cannon estimates his income at more than $800,000 in 1975. His goal was not just to make money but also to energize the right and create a groundswell for his presidential campaign. He talked about revitalizing the GOP as a conservative force that could succeed by "raising a banner of no pale pastels but bold colors which make it unmistakably clear where we stand on all the issues troubling the people." This optimism, as always, was one of his most appealing traits.

But Reagan's presidential campaign started with a misstep. He delivered a speech on September 26, 1975, to the Executive Club of Chicago calling for a massive shift in power and responsibility from Washington to the states, municipalities, and private sector. Ford's strategists, inspired by Stuart Spencer, who had defected from Reagan to Ford, pounced on the speech and said Reagan's plan would savage many cherished federal programs, including education and job training, regional development, transportation, law enforcement, Medicaid, and other health programs by cutting federal outlays by $90 billion. Reagan was portrayed in the media as an extremist—Barry Goldwater redux.

Ford narrowly won the New Hampshire primary as 1976 began, then won the March 9 primary in Florida as his surrogates raised questions about Reagan's age (sixty-five) and portrayed him as a right-wing zealot for saying that Social Security could be made voluntary. By March 16 Reagan had been defeated in New Hampshire and Illinois and did not contest Ford in Massachusetts and Vermont.

But the former California governor would not relent in his message. He stepped up his attacks on the incumbent, mentioning him by name, which violated his own "Eleventh Commandment" not to speak ill of another Republican.

One wedge issue was whether the United States should turn over the Panama Canal to Panama. In opposing the transfer, Reagan played on conservatives' resentment at losing the Vietnam War and the sense that the United States was being pushed around by second-rate powers. Reagan struck a chord when he called Panamanian leader Omar Torrijos a "tinhorn dictator."

On March 23 Reagan won the North Carolina primary, in part by emphasizing his opposition to Ford's proposed "give-away" of the Panama Canal. "We bought it, we paid for it, it's ours, and we're going to keep it," Reagan declared. He also attacked Ford for running up the biggest federal budget deficit in history and for allegedly losing military superiority to the Soviet Union. More important, he inspired his party's voters with his dream of America as "a shining city on the hill" and mankind's last, best hope, while Ford appeared lackluster and lacking in ideas.

The combination of Reagan's optimism and his hard-hitting attacks on Ford ignited a wave of conservative animus toward the incumbent, who had never been popular with his party's

Ronald Reagan at the California Republican Party Convention, 1979.

right wing. The challenger had finally succeeded in energizing conservative zealots and inspiring them to turn out at the polls. Suddenly Reagan caught fire. He won 45 percent of the vote in Wisconsin, took all 96 delegates in the Texas primary on May 1, and won 130 of 139 delegates at stake in Alabama, Georgia, and Indiana. He won Nebraska May 11, with Ford managing a win in West Virginia, and then Reagan captured California. As the Republican National Convention approached, Reagan and Ford were running neck and neck. In the end, Ford won 1,187 delegates to Reagan's 1,070, enough to narrowly lock up the nomination.

But Ford went down to defeat at the hands of Democrat Jimmy Carter in November, leaving Reagan in an excellent position for 1980.

❧ ❧ ❧

"I paid for this microphone, Mr. Green!"

The 1980 campaign unfolded amid a backdrop of extraordinary national self-doubt symbolized by the Iranian hostage crisis. Fifty-two American citizens had been seized by radical Muslims and held captive for more than a year in Teheran. The hostages were repeatedly paraded before television cameras and humiliated, while Carter remained powerless to free them. A rescue attempt was badly botched in the desert, adding to the administration's ineffectual image. Just as important, inflation was at historic levels, and unemployment was causing severe pain throughout the country. Through it all, Carter projected a dour and pessimistic image, seeming to blame Americans for a national malaise that many attributed to Carter's own failure of leadership.

Reagan told friends there was nothing wrong with America that good sense and a dose of self-confidence could not make right. Recalling his earlier days when everything seemed possible in the world's greatest democracy, he felt he was on a mission to restore America's "greatness."

Reagan began the 1980 campaign as the front-runner for the GOP nomination. When he announced his candidacy in New York on November 13, 1979, questions about his age, his vitality, and his knowledge of the issues were his first obstacles. He quickly showed that he had the energy to compete, crisscrossing the country by air at a hectic pace, but he was woefully unprepared on the issues. He even bollixed up answers to questions from reporters on federal aid to New York—the most predictable questions of all, given the site of his announcement in the city itself. He lost the Iowa precinct caucuses to George Bush on January 21, 1980, with Bush taking 33 percent of the vote to Reagan's 30 percent, and that ended Reagan's strategy of campaigning as the front-runner, removed from contact with everyday voters.

A turning point came at a debate February 23 in Nashua, New Hampshire. Reagan's organizers agreed to pay the costs of the encounter, and he invited four other GOP candidates to participate, not just Bush, his main rival. When Bush appeared on the dais and opposed including the additional competitors, Reagan tried to explain why the others should be allowed to participate. It was part of a calculated strategy to diminish Bush by not letting him take Reagan on one-on-one. Suddenly, Jon Breen, the moderator, interrupted and instructed technicians, "Turn Mr. Reagan's microphone off." Reagan replied angrily: "I paid for this microphone, Mr. Green [sic]!" The

Ronald Reagan arrives on home turf in California during his 1980 campaign.

face-off showed Reagan in control, a dominating presence. Three days later, on February 26, he took 51 percent of the vote; Bush finished a poor second, with 22 percent. Theatrics had helped win the day.

On the afternoon of his New Hampshire win, Reagan demonstrated decisiveness in another way by firing his imperious campaign manager, John Sears, along with aides Charles Black and James Lake. Nancy Reagan, it turned out, had been a prime mover in the shake-up, which involved the installation of William J. Casey as the new campaign manager. She told her husband that Sears and his aides were not letting "Reagan be Reagan" by keeping him away from voters and isolating him from longtime friends and confidants on the campaign staff. She also argued that Sears had been wasting money with unnecessary expenditures.

From then on, Reagan rolled to the nomination with ease. At the GOP convention he picked Bush as his running mate after briefly considering Gerald Ford in a "dream ticket." (Reagan decided that choosing Ford, the former president, as his No. 2 would inevitably lead to questions about who was ultimately in charge, so he rejected the idea.)

Reagan's debate with President Carter on October 28 in Cleveland locked up Reagan's victory. He was smooth but tough, self-deprecating but knowledgeable. His put-down of Carter with the remark "There you go again" summed up a common view of the incumbent as self-righteous. And by asking the country, "Are you better off today than you were four years ago?" Reagan posed precisely the right question. He turned the election into a referendum on Carter's perceived lack of leadership and his four troubled years as president, diverting attention from himself.

❧   ❧   ❧

". . . I'm one of them."

As the magnitude of his victory became clear on Election Day, Reagan was asked what Americans saw in him. "Would you laugh if I told you that I think, maybe, they see themselves and that I'm one of them?" he replied. "I've never been able to detach myself or think that I, somehow, am apart from them."

Reagan cast his ballot near his home in Pacific Palisades and then went to a barbershop for a haircut, the perfect Middle American touch for Election Day news coverage. Superstitious about claiming victory prematurely, he refused to predict the outcome for reporters. He was taking a shower before dinner when the TV networks reported that he had won big in the

Northeast and the South; at 5:15 P.M. Pacific time, the networks projected that Ronald Wilson Reagan would be elected the fortieth president by an overwhelming margin. He would win with nearly 44 million votes or 50.7 percent and 489 electoral votes; Carter got 35.5 million votes or 41 percent and only 44 electoral votes; independent John Anderson won 5.7 million votes or 6.6 percent, with no electoral votes.

That evening, the Reagans had a quiet dinner with friends and aides at the Bel Air mansion of Earle Jorgensen, a businessman who had helped him run for governor so long ago. Afterward, the president-elect and his wife retired to a top-floor suite at the nearby Century Plaza Hotel to make phone calls thanking friends and supporters.

Reagan pollster Richard Wirthlin, who had accurately predicted the outcome, said the election represented a historic opportunity for the conservative movement. It could be a turning point, Wirthlin said, perhaps the end of Franklin Roosevelt's New Deal coalition that had included big-city ethnic groups, white Southerners, blacks, union members, and the bulk of the middle class. This remained to be seen.

For his part, Reagan was happy but neither awed nor humbled. He saw his victory as less a personal triumph than the simple result of the people's will; he was only their instrument. His sense of destiny would be intensified the following March, when he came face-to-face with his own mortality.

Neil Reagan shook his brother's hand on Election Night and said, "I bet there's a hot time in Dixon tonight."

"I'd like to be there off in a corner just listening," replied the president-elect, the small-town boy who never forgot his roots.

When he took office just before turning seventy, he became the oldest man ever to serve as president, but he was poised to give official Washington a new brand of vibrant leadership that exploited the medium of television as never before.

"By the time Reagan reached the stage of the White House, he had more experience pleasing audiences than any American politician since William Jennings Bryan," wrote historian James David Barber. "He had mastered the arts of dramatic performance on the stage, in radio sportscasting and commentary, in the movies, in television, and in specialized and general platform oratory. . . . And not since [President Warren] Harding had a happy-talk President's character and style fit together so nicely with the public's yearning for positive thinking in politics. . . .

"The obvious combination of public personality and media talent made it surprising that it had taken so long for the Reagan type to appear in the age of media politics. . . . Painted by his opposition as a combination fool and knave, he knew how to turn those expectations to his advantage; he became one of those lucky politicians who get credit for being normal."

And a sense of normalcy is what Americans desperately wanted as the Reagan era began.

circa 1981

CHAPTER FIVE

PRESIDENT: FIRST TERM

From the moment he took the oath of office on the clear, unseasonably warm morning of January 20, 1981, Ronald Reagan established an optimistic, can-do approach to the presidency. His message was a dramatic contrast to the angst-ridden air that had surrounded Jimmy Carter.

"We have every right to dream heroic dreams," Reagan declared in his inaugural address. ". . . We're not, as some would have us believe, doomed to an inevitable decline. I do not believe in a fate that will fall on us no matter what we do. I do believe in a fate that will fall on us if we do nothing."

Reagan's optimism was severely tested from the start. One of his main goals was to banish the fear that was nagging many Americans, reeling from inflation and double-digit unemployment at home and repeated humiliations for the United States abroad, that the presidency was too big a job for one person. But the Democratic establishment in Washington was not ready to cooperate. When, as president-elect, he met with House Speaker Thomas "Tip" O'Neill on November 18, 1980, O'Neill told Reagan that his experience as governor of California was "minor-league." Legislation might come easily in Sacramento, the Speaker lectured, but in Washington passing bills would be a much more difficult task. "This is the big leagues," O'Neill declared.

Yet "Reagan was the first guy since [Harry] Truman who was comfortable with himself," said Michael Deaver, Reagan's first-term media adviser. "Ronald Reagan had it figured out. You felt his feet were on the ground and he knew where he was going." Even though his philosophy was conservative, Reagan had no qualms about breaking all the supposed rules of the presidency, and he operated much as he had as governor of California.

First, Reagan never believed the presidency required herculean amounts of time and energy, so he took a nine-to-five approach to his job. He delegated freely—his critics said too freely—to talented subordinates, setting the overall themes and letting aides do the rest. As the oldest man ever elected president up to that time, he was careful not to overtax himself. He took naps in the afternoons, allowed himself long weekends at Camp David, and spent weeks in seclusion at his Santa Barbara ranch. In general, Reagan resigned himself to seclusion with far more ease than most presidents. Partly it was his age; old men are not as likely to make a habit of trips to the movies or fashionable restaurants as younger people, and Reagan had no young children in the White House to accompany to ball games or school recitals. Mike Deaver came upon Reagan in a pensive moment one Saturday shortly after he took office. The new president was standing at a window on the third-floor White House residence, looking out over Lafayette Park and down Sixteenth Street.

"You know," Reagan said, "I'll never be able to do that."

"What?" Deaver asked.

"Walk out of here to a bookstore," Reagan said. "To just do it alone."

He was right, but it didn't seem to bother him that much. His idea of a pleasant evening was to have dinner with Nancy in the White House residence, often on tray tables with the television tuned to a vintage movie, or "Dallas" or "Dynasty," two popular melodramas that celebrated wealth and power.

At the same time, Reagan was far from unaware that he needed to dispel doubts that he was too old for his job and that he lacked the vigor to be an effective president. He tackled the issue head-on, with self-deprecating humor.

One of his favorite and best-received one-liners—told in a variety of ways—openly made fun of his advancing years. In his State of the Union address on January 26, 1982, he told the nation: "President Washington began this tradition in 1790 after reminding the nation that the destiny of self-government and the 'preservation of the sacred fire of liberty' is 'finally staked on the experiment entrusted to the hands of the American people.' For our friends in the press, who place a high premium on accuracy, let me say, I did not actually hear George Washington say that."

He told the Oklahoma legislature on March 16, 1982: "I appreciate having this opportunity to speak with you during the seventy-fifth year of your statehood. And it's not true that I was in the original land rush."

It was hokey and silly, but it served to defuse an issue that could have damaged Reagan's ability to lead the nation.

Just as important to his management of national affairs, Reagan had learned some important lessons about administration over the years. He did not delegate excessive authority to a single aide, as he had done initially as governor and as a presidential candidate. He saw himself as the chairman of the board of a huge corporation, and he began by dividing responsibilities among a troika of aides: James Baker as chief of staff and top administrator, Ed Meese as presidential counselor and keeper of the conservative flame, and Michael Deaver as architect of his image. Baker, Meese, and Deaver would meet each morning over breakfast, and gather again each evening to discuss the events of the day, long after Reagan had returned to the White House residence. To a considerable degree, it was the troika that ensured the successes of the administration at the start.

His kitchen cabinet, though influential, was no longer the force it had been in California. Reagan was now confident in his own abilities and in the skills of his troika and did not need the outsiders for advice anymore.

"Reagan sits at any gathering of close advisers as an interested participant rather than as the leader who orders the discussion," said John Sears, who had worked closely with Reagan during the campaign but was fired after the New Hampshire primary. "He's not a stupid man. He appreciates the nuances of what is proposed to him. It's just that he's not the originator of ideas. He's a more malleable and moderate person than he's generally thought to be. He's not a conceptualizer. He's a borrower and an endorser. It's fair to say that on some occasions he is presented with options and selects one, but it is also true that in other instances he simply looks to someone to tell him what to do."

As mentioned earlier, Reagan had learned to be "handled" and "managed" while he was an actor; it worked for him then, and he was always comfortable with stage-management, role-playing, and scripting.

Yet Reagan friends and associates insisted that, while this

consensus approach was part of Reagan's personality, he also could be stubborn and would overrule his aides without qualm if he felt strongly enough about a course of action. This stubborn side of the new president would show through just as clearly as his consensus-minded side over the years on issues ranging from his opposition to income-tax increases to his final rapprochement with Mikhail Gorbachev in the mid-1980s.

Reagan also put his life experiences to good use. He never forgot his essentially pleasant upbringing in Dixon, Illinois, and he came to believe that his small-town experiences represented the quintessential American life that could be replicated even in today's sophisticated society. He had spent considerable time pondering what he would do with power, and his answer was to set a clear direction for the country by emphasizing three objectives: tax cuts, less government, and a strong national defense. These became his mantras.

During the campaign, he had become entranced with the theories of "supply-side economists" led by Arthur Laffer of the University of Southern California. Reagan adopted those ideas, and they became known as "Reaganomics." The goal was to balance the federal budget, cut income taxes, and increase defense spending, all at the same time. These, of course, seemed to be contradictory, but the reasoning was that cuts in tax rates would trigger a vast economic expansion that would, in turn, bring in more tax revenue through a combination of lower interest rates, less inflation, more business expansion, and more jobs. Such Panglossian theories appealed to Reagan's desire for simple, painless panaceas. Even some of his senior advisers had strong doubts about his economic ideas. David Stockman, his first budget director, admitted privately that the administration's program was a "Trojan horse" designed to hide old-fashioned trickle-down economics in which those at the top of the economic ladder got the most benefits, and gains would then "trickle down" to Americans on the lower rungs.

Like most presidents, Reagan decided that his success would depend on how much he accomplished at the beginning of his tenure, when he could exploit to the fullest the voters' mandate. And it was clear that, no matter how many economists warned that Reagan's program would vastly balloon the deficit, most Americans liked "Reaganomics." A poll taken by *The Washington Post* and ABC News in mid-February found two-to-one support for Reagan's program, especially the tax cuts.

Despite his reputation as a disengaged manager with lackadaisical work habits, he was full of energy when it came to promoting his economic agenda. Not only did he appeal directly and repeatedly to the country on television, he also lobbied individual members of Congress constantly, holding 69 meetings with 467 legislators during his first 100 days. He was particularly successful in wooing conservative Democrats from the South, known as "boll weevils," to join Republicans to support his legislation. In pushing for these goals, he stage-managed the presidency more than had ever been done before, scripting even the tiniest details for television and carrying it off with an actor's aplomb.

His policies often seemed ignorant and mean-spirited. Of particular concern were his repeated attempts to cut back the social safety net of programs designed to guarantee assistance to the unfortunate. When his administration tried to declare ketchup a vegetable in order to reduce federal outlays for lunches, critics were outraged. His penchant for associating with the rich and glamorous, especially his old millionaire California pals, made him seem preoccupied with creating a culture of superficiality and greed.

But his affable manner and sunny disposition drew respect even from those who disagreed with him, such as New York governor Mario Cuomo, who praised Reagan's bravery during the crucible he endured that year.

❦ ❦ ❦

"Honey, I forgot to duck."

On March 30, 1981, Reagan was emerging from a speech at the Washington Hilton Hotel when a deranged drifter named John Hinckley Jr. fired six shots at the president. One explosive "Devastator" bullet ricocheted off Reagan's limousine and slit his side under his left armpit like a knife, lodging within an inch of his heart.

White House press secretary Jim Brady was hit in the head, suffering permanent brain damage. Secret Service agent Timothy J. McCarthy and Washington policeman Thomas K. Delehanty also suffered serious wounds. Secret Service agent Jerry Parr pushed the president into the waiting limousine a few feet away, ramming Reagan's head against the outside of the car, and the agent fell on top of him on the floor of the rear compartment. Then the vehicle sped away.

When the president arrived at George Washington University Hospital, his vital signs were weak and Secret Service agents were eager to rush him into the emergency room. But Reagan balked. He got out of the limousine, straightened his shoulders, buttoned up his suit jacket, then walked stiffly through the hospital doorway on his own. Once inside, he fell to one knee and stumbled into the emergency room with the assistance of several agents.

Reagan refused to show a loss of dignity or what he consid-

The aftermath: Secret service agents, with weapons out, tackle gunman John Hinckley Jr. as White House press secretary James Brady lies critically wounded nearby on the sidewalk, March 30, 1981.

ered unpresidential behavior; the old Hollywood actor would not diminish the best role of his life. "He believed it was part of the role of the president of the United States to show strength and confidence to the American people," former White House media adviser Michael Deaver told me later. "You never saw weakness."

Reagan's grace and sense of humor inspired the country. When he first saw Nancy at the hospital, he grinned and said, "Honey, I forgot to duck" (a quip similar to the one boxer Jack Dempsey had told his wife after losing the heavyweight championship to Gene Tunney in 1926, when Reagan was fifteen).

As doctors prepared him for surgery, he said, "Please tell me you're Republicans." As he rested in the recovery room, he wrote on a notepad, "All in all, I'd rather be in Philadelphia" (a reprise of a famous line by comedian W. C. Fields).

The assassination attempt convinced the nation of Reagan's courage and, when he recovered in a short time, of his physical vigor. It convinced Reagan of his destiny. "God saved me for a purpose," he told a confidant. He came to believe his destiny was to somehow stop communism and restore America's "greatness."

Propelled by public support, Reagan pushed ahead with what was known as the "Kemp-Roth bill," named after Representative Jack Kemp of New York and Senator Bill Roth of Delaware, Republicans who favored income-tax cuts of 10 percent a year for three years. Stockman won congressional support by developing phantom budget savings and making rosy economic predictions that fudged over the deficit increases that Reagan's program was bound to generate.

In the end, Reagan won congressional approval for a plan that was more modest than what he had promised but retained the core principles on which he had campaigned: a 5 percent income-tax cut to take effect on October 1, 1981, to be followed by a 10 percent cut on July 1, 1982, and another 10 percent cut on July 1, 1983. He increased military spending by $28 billion, the largest boost in peacetime history. He won approval for cuts in many social programs, including college education benefits, public service jobs under the Comprehensive Employment and Training Act, child nutrition, unemployment compensation, the growth of Medicare, welfare, and food stamps. It amounted to a large shift in spending from social programs to the Pentagon.

In months, Reagan had changed the nature of America's

⬥ PATCO ⬥

PRESIDENT REAGAN AT AN AUGUST 1981 BRIEFING WITH TRANSPORTATION SECRETARY DREW LEWIS, RIGHT, AND ATTORNEY GENERAL WILLIAM FRENCH SMITH.

One of Reagan's defining moments was his dismissal of 11,400 striking air traffic controllers in the summer of 1981, six months after he took office and only four months after the assassination attempt that nearly took his life.

Reagan had a lot to prove—that he was capable of decisive action in a crisis, that he was not willing to succumb to pressure from special interests, and that he was still vigorous enough to do his job. The perfect opportunity arose when the Professional Air Traffic Controllers' Organization (PATCO) struck illegally in August 1981 and tied up air travel across the country and to some extent around the world.

An angry Reagan fired the controllers within forty-eight hours of the start of their strike, which had been prompted when the government failed to meet PATCO's demands for higher pay and better working conditions.

Reagan argued that, since the strike was illegal, the controllers automatically had forfeited their jobs by walking out.

More important than the legal issues, Reagan used the occasion to show that he was "a tough, determined president who would uphold the law and, unlike his predecessor, would not be pushed around by grasping interest groups," wrote political scientist Bruce Miroff. "The spectacle also conveyed to organized labor that the White House knew how to feed popular suspicions of unions and could make things difficult for a labor movement that became too assertive."

The result was that PATCO was broken as a union and Reagan's popularity soared.

political and social debate. "That debate will not take, as an automatic 'given,' the position that government spending can solve most of our social problems," presidential pollster Richard Wirthlin said in March 1982, after the Reagan revolution had established itself. "The federal government will likely be viewed by Republicans and Democrats alike as functioning in a world of limits just as the rest of us do." Wirthlin was correct. Six months after losing two budget fights to Reagan, Tip O'Neill was asked by a constituent what was going on. "I'm getting the shit kicked out of me," was his reply.

Yet Reagan was unwilling to fully take on the popular entitlement programs, especially Social Security and Medicare, which most economists agreed were the key to restraining the growth of domestic spending. These were programs to which any American was entitled if he or she met a basic standard of eligibility. Entitlement costs had spiraled upward at a dramatic rate—from $70 billion in 1970 to $295 billion in 1981. But Reagan decided that he would not risk his reelection by attacking those programs, so he mostly left them alone. The approach did nothing to cut the deficit, and Reagan refused to address the problem for eight years.

❖ ❖ ❖

"Stay the course."

The biggest test of Reagan's resolve came in 1982, when recession was cutting deeply into the country's well-being. Reagan's critics blamed him for making the nation's problems worse, or at least for failing to take action to comfort Americans riven by economic distress.

Inflation had slowed, but more than 10,000 companies went

bankrupt between January and November 1981, a 48 percent increase from a year earlier. Unemployment increased to 10 percent, the highest percentage since 1940, and in poor inner cities and some rural areas the jobless rate reached 30 or 40 percent.

Meanwhile, the Reagan administration, with the acceptance of Congress, imposed a package of non-income-tax increases and cut 300,000 poor persons from jobs under the Comprehensive Employment and Training Act in 1982. Reagan also cut welfare programs and halted disability insurance payments under Social Security for nearly 110,000 families, and his appointees weakened standards for mine safety, food and drug regulation, air and water quality, and toxic-waste cleanup. Economist Robert Reich (who would become secretary of labor under President Bill Clinton in 1993) found in September 1982 that in the previous year 661,000 children lost coverage under Medicaid, the federal health-care program for the poor; 900,000 poor children no longer received free or reduced-price breakfast; 150,000 poor working families lost eligibility for government-supported day care; and 1 million persons were dropped from the food-stamp program.

Throughout all this, Reagan defended his economic program under the slogan "Stay the course." It caused the Republicans serious losses in the midterm elections of 1982, but the president would not back down. He clung stubbornly to the belief that if it was necessary to increase the deficit in order to break the back of communism through astronomical defense spending, it was worth the price. But he also believed that eventually supply-side economics would prove itself and the deficit would begin to decline; this, of course, never happened.

Some of the Washington cognoscenti began deriding him as a one-term president, and Democrats ranging from former vice president Walter Mondale to Colorado senator Gary Hart began lining up to run against him.

Yet even during the dark days of the 1981–82 recession, Reagan's critics grudgingly admitted that his personality was mitigating the flaws in his policies, and they dubbed him "the Teflon president" because nothing stuck to him. "He's cutting the heart out of the American dream to own a home and have a good job and still he's popular," complained House Speaker Tip O'Neill. The Democratic leader added in late 1981: "People like him as an individual, and he handles the media better than anybody since Franklin Roosevelt, even including Jack Kennedy. There's just something about the guy that people like. They want him to be a success. They're rooting for him and of course they're rooting for him because we haven't had any presidential successes for years—Kennedy killed, Johnson with Vietnam, Nixon with Watergate, Ford, Carter. . . ."

Perhaps one reason for that support was one of Reagan's strengths as a politician and a leader: He tried to keep his campaign promises. While his most important pledge, of course, was to cut taxes and boost defense spending, and he pursued that course aggressively, there had been other promises as well. On July 7, 1981, he nominated Arizona state Court of Appeals judge Sandra Day O'Connor to the U.S. Supreme Court, redeeming his pledge to do all he could to name the first woman justice; she would be confirmed easily later that year. And as he had promised, he lifted a grain embargo against the USSR, which he felt had hurt U.S. farmers more than the Soviets. He set about curbing the size and power of Washington by reducing regulations and attempting to do away with whole functions of the federal government, such as the Department of Education and the Department of Energy (though he failed to convince Congress to abolish either). And he moved to devolve power to the states, to the municipalities, and to the private sector.

Reagan had also promised to slow the "deluge" of Japanese cars into the U.S. market, a trend that was decimating the already weakened American auto industry. This protectionist pledge, of course, took much of the edge off his longtime commitment to free trade, shared by Treasury secretary Donald Regan, budget director David Stockman, and Murray Weidenbaum, chairman of the Council of Economic Advisers. In May 1982 after bitter internal wrangling in Washington, the administration pressured the Japanese to accept "voluntary restraints" on their exports of vehicles into the United States—a victory of pragmatists over free traders, but also a redemption of Reagan's campaign promise.

When cornered, Reagan was surprisingly nimble. The proposed MX intercontinental ballistic missile provided a difficult challenge precisely because it inextricably linked foreign policy with the domestic matters and political concerns that Reagan considered most important. Further complicating the issue was the fact that Reagan started out less hawkish about the MX than Carter had been, and when he became president it was one of the most vexing issues he faced.

The MX was designed to deter the Soviet Union from launching a nuclear first strike against the West. Carter wanted to build 200 of the huge missiles, supposedly capable of pinpoint accuracy, and install them underground in the deserts of Nevada and Utah. The plan was to continuously shuttle the MX missiles on railcars along a vast complex of tunnels that connected 4,600 shelters; such constant movement along an underground "racetrack" would prevent Moscow from destroying all the missiles in a surprise attack, so the United States could always wipe out Soviet civilization in a counterattack. Yet the racetrack-and-shelter system would enable international inspectors to verify the number of MX missiles under a then-planned strategic arms limitation treaty called SALT II. In 1981 the cost was estimated at more than $50 billion, far more than the $33 billion Carter had forecast.

Reagan had many objections to the plan. He thought the racetrack idea was too expensive and would take too much land from western ranchers, some of his primary constituents. He believed that environmentalists would tie up the land transfers for years with hostile lawsuits, undermining the deterrent value of the whole scheme. And he was troubled when leaders of the Church of Jesus Christ of Latter-Day Saints (Mormons) announced in May 1981 that the MX system ran directly counter to their commitment to peace on earth. The vast majority of Utah's population was Mormon; both of its senators were Republicans and strong Reagan backers, and Utah had given Reagan his biggest majority of any state in 1980.

Reagan's senior advisers argued among themselves for many weeks, but the final compromise, which the president accepted in late 1981, was a political masterstroke, if suspect in military terms. The United States would start building MX missiles, Reagan announced, but he said a permanent basing decision would be delayed until more research was done; 40 of the missiles would be placed in existing silos for other missiles; the silos would be "superhardened" to protect against Soviet attack (though it was doubtful that such "hardening" would work). The scheme, developed largely by Defense secretary Caspar Weinberger and that Reagan understood only at the most rudimentary level, managed to defuse the critics of the racetrack plan and at the same time demonstrate internationally that the new administration was taking a tough stand on defense. The next year, in 1982, Congress halted MX missile production until a basing decision was made. Eventually the program was abandoned as relations between the superpowers began to improve.

❖ ❖ ❖

"... weakness can be provocative"

Early in Reagan's first term, though, any prospect of improving superpower relations seemed remote. Reagan was, quite simply, regarded as dangerously bellicose.

Journalist Hedrick Smith wrote that there were two Ronald Reagans, one pragmatic, one ideological: "One Reagan is the rhetorical right-winger who instinctively voices wide popular disenchantment with postwar American diplomacy, who conveys the sense that the world is a dangerous and inhospitable place, and utters resentment that America has retreated in the face of Soviet advances. This is the Reagan of confrontation. . . . The other Reagan is the pragmatic practitioner of power. His statements are more circumspect, his language more carefully ambiguous and qualified. If the right-wing Reagan urges a blockade of Cuba, the pragmatic Reagan shrewdly refuses to be lured into advocating American intervention in Iran. . . . This is the Reagan of accommodation, who talks of a 'reasonable and balanced' relationship with Russia."

During his first four years, Reagan was one-sidedly confrontational; he retreated to Cold War rhetoric and saw virtually every international problem as an extension of the East-West struggle. He refused to recognize that many localized conflicts stemmed from purely regional dynamics—factors such as ethnic and religious hatreds that were much more relevant than communism in many areas, such as the Middle East, southern Africa, Northern Ireland, and large parts of Asia.

For Reagan, foreign policy revolved around strengthening America's military forces, in particular by modernizing the nuclear arsenal, and trying to use the threat of a new, vastly expensive arms race to pressure the Soviets into making both military and diplomatic concessions.

He warned of the dangers of appeasement and saw the Soviet invasion of Afghanistan and Soviet involvement in successful Marxist insurrections in Angola, Ethiopia, and South Yemen (which had occurred during Carter's presidency) as evidence that Moscow did not respect Washington's resolve. "World War II came about without provocation," he said. "It came because nations were weak, not strong, in the face of aggression. Those same lessons of the past surely apply today. Firmness based on a strong defense capability is not provocative. But weakness can be provocative simply because it is tempting to a nation whose imperialist ambitions are virtually unlimited. We find ourselves increasingly in a position of dangerous isolation. Our allies are losing confidence in us, and our adversaries no longer respect us."

He said on another occasion, "The Soviet Union underlies all the unrest that is going on. If they weren't engaged in this game of dominoes, there wouldn't be any hot spots in the world." He also said he believed in linking arms negotiations to Soviet behavior around the globe, which Jimmy Carter had abandoned in the interests of moving toward what he considered the higher good of nuclear arms control.

One of the administration's most controversial initiatives was known as the Reagan Doctrine: supporting anti-Communist insurgencies in the Third World through both overt

GRENADA

AMERICAN TROOPS IN
GRENADA, 1983.

Reagan boosted his popularity again in October 1983 when he ordered American troops to invade the tiny Caribbean island of Grenada.

The president had been embarrassed that the Marxist regime of Grenada's ruler, Maurice Bishop, was cozying up to Cuba, and he began to consider sending in the Marines when radical Marxists murdered Bishop and took power, threatening to immediately intensify ties with Havana. The Organization of Eastern Caribbean States—the governments of other islands surrounding Grenada—urged the United States to intervene.

And White House officials quickly realized that there was another rationale for action: the need to protect a small band of students stranded at a medical school not far outside the capital of St. George's as well as other Americans remaining on the island.

U.S. troops, who outnumbered the tiny Grenadian army by ten to one, made short work of the invasion and evacuated the Americans. U.S. officials then announced that the American troops had found large amounts of military equipment and papers indicating that Cuba was planning to turn Grenada into a base for exporting communism and terrorism thoughout the region—claims that critics later showed were dubious.

Yet Reagan made what was essentially a minor event into a public-relations triumph; after all the island contained only 100,000 residents and a territory of only 133 square miles and the invasion had no lasting diplomatic or military significance. But Reagan was portrayed by his aides as being firmly in charge, and photos were released of him dressed in bathrobe and slippers as he listened to a briefing by senior officials. Reagan also demonized the ruling regime as "a brutal group of leftist thugs," imbuing the invasion with righteousness in the minds of many Americans.

Journalists were barred from covering the landings, just in case something went wrong and to avoid photos and stories about dead or wounded Americans and civilians. Upon returning home, several U.S. students kissed the tarmac at the airport and praised Reagan for decisive leadership that saved their lives. And the Grenadian people seemed overjoyed that the United States had freed them.

The rest of the world did not seem as pleased. The USSR and many Latin American governments condemned the military action and even the French and British expressed

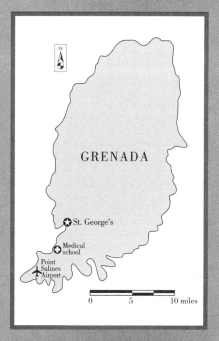

concern, if not outrage. The UN Security Council approved a resolution deploring the invasion.

Reagan was not deterred, though. "Our days of weakness are over," the president declared. "Our military forces are back on their feet and standing tall."

But the overriding political point was that Ronald Reagan, the easygoing newcomer from the West, had ridden to the rescue in the nick of time. Polls showed that 63 percent of the voters approved of his job performance, his highest rating up to that point in his presidency.

and covert means. In implementing this change, Reagan reversed U.S. policy dating back to the late 1940s, which had been to contain Soviet expansion. Instead, he sought to roll back communism in areas where unpopular governments were propped up by the USSR or by Soviet clients such as Cuba.

The results were mixed. In the end, the Soviets pulled out of Afghanistan, and the Vietnamese began withdrawing from Cambodia. And Reagan eliminated a left-wing dictatorship in Grenada when, on October 25, 1983, he ordered Marines and Army Rangers to invade the tiny Caribbean island after the leftist government of Prime Minister Maurice Bishop was ousted by more extreme members of his own party.

In El Salvador, the United States sent huge amounts of military and economic aid to the Christian Democratic government of José Napoleon Duarte, which was being besieged by the left. In Angola, the administration provided covert military aid to Jonas Savimbi's anti-Communist rebel force known as the National Union for the Total Independence of Angola (UNITA). The Reagan administration also conducted repeated military operations against Libya and its ruler, Colonel Muammar el-Qaddafi, which the administration believed had sponsored worldwide terrorism.

But it was in Nicaragua that Reagan made one of his most controversial commitments when his administration sent money and arms and provided training to rebel Contras, who were attempting to overthrow the Marxist government known as the Sandinistas. Reagan met the Contra leaders several times at the White House and established a personal bond with them. He romanticized their struggle as a case of good versus evil, comparing the Contras to America's Founding Fathers and declaring that Nicaragua was in danger of becoming a Soviet state in America's backyard.

Congress, pushed by majority Democrats in the House who considered the whole enterprise perilously similar to U.S. involvement in Vietnam, tried to block him. In Reagan's first term, the legislators passed the Boland Amendment, banning any expenditure of funds to overthrow the Nicaragua regime. But Reagan would not give up; he jousted with Congress over these questions until the Iran-Contra scandal erupted in the fall of 1986 and tainted the Reagan Doctrine for the rest of his term.

His views hardened further when the Soviets shot down Korean Air Lines (KAL) flight 007 on August 31, 1983. All 269 persons aboard, including many Americans, were killed. Moscow at first tried to deny any knowledge of the downing of the civilian airliner, which was flying from Alaska to Seoul and had strayed 300 miles off course, entering Soviet airspace for unknown reasons.

Reagan reacted with admirable caution, refusing to move hastily, and rejecting his aides' advice to impose harsh sanctions on Moscow for what was a case of mistaken identity. Instead, Reagan responded in a measured and careful manner: He canceled the renewal of a transportation agreement with Moscow, and he condemned the Soviets in moral terms. In a nationally televised speech from the Oval Office on September 5, Reagan called the shoot-down a "massacre" and an "atrocity" and a "crime against humanity." Moscow, meanwhile, called the KAL flight a U.S. spy mission.

Despite his cautious response, the KAL flight deepened Reagan's conviction that the Communists in Moscow, under their leader, Yuri Andropov, were a wicked and callous regime, and tension between the two sides got so bad that Pope John Paul II warned publicly that the superpowers might be heading for a "new prewar phase." Reagan seemed to confirm such fears when, in a radio address on September 17, he said, "We may not be able to change the Soviets' ways, but we can change our attitude toward them. . . . We can stop pretending they share the same dreams and aspirations we do. We can start preparing ourselves for what John F. Kennedy called a long twilight struggle."

Reagan's belief in showing American resolve through military force was a centerpiece of his foreign policy, but it led him to overreach. One of his worst reverses occurred just before 6:30 A.M. on the quiet Sunday of October 23, 1983, when the bombing of a U.S. Marines compound at Beirut International Airport killed 241 Americans and called into question his policy of armed engagement in the world's trouble spots.

Particularly embarrassing for Reagan were the questions that the bombing raised about the security of American soldiers, which the hawkish Reaganites had lambasted the Democrats for weakening. A single suicide driver, it turned out, had maneuvered an explosives-filled truck inside the perimeter of the Marine compound without detection. The terrorist, who was killed in the blast, drove the truck over a roll of barbed wire and past two Marine sentry posts without being fired upon, then crossed eighty-nine yards of open parking lot, ramming through a fence and a wooden sentry hut. The vehicle crashed into the headquarters building, detonating 2,000 pounds of explosives in the atrium lobby. The blast left a crater 30 feet deep and 40 feet across.

The losses caused Reagan to reevaluate his policy of sending U.S. troops to keep the peace in Lebanon. Soon after, he pulled out the Marines.

It was no wonder that Reagan preferred to devote himself to matters closer to home, even though, as the recession of 1981–82 deepened, his popularity continued to sink. Only 35 percent of the voters approved of his job performance at midterm, and the Republicans lost 26 seats in the House of Representatives in the 1982 elections.

❖ ❖ ❖

"*The camera doesn't lie.*"

How did his presidency survive this dark period? In addition to his buoyant, likable personality, in many ways it was how that personality was presented that helped make him "the Teflon president." In fact, he stage-managed the presidency as never before, bringing the White House fully into the television age as he proved that he deserved the nickname: "The Great Communicator."

"Ronald Reagan used to tell me, 'The camera doesn't lie,' " recalled his White House media adviser, Michael Deaver, in 1995. And as a veteran actor, he used television far better than any of his predecessors. Much of his success was because of his mellifluous voice, which was capable of whispery softness to convey sincerity and a crisp emphasis on punchy lines to project forcefulness when necessary. Just as important, the White House fed the TV networks a constant diet of vivid and dramatic visuals, all designed to flatter the president.

Deaver told me in 1995, "I have always believed that impressions are more important than specific acts or issues, especially with the president. . . . I believe TV is a great boon to us in judging our leaders. It lets us see all the dimensions that, in the past, people could only see in person: the body language, the dilation of the eye, the way they perspire. We see them when they are tired, worried, under great crises. If television focuses on somebody every day [as it does with any president], it shows all the dimensions."

Reagan's press policies were based on three tenets: Limit direct access to the president; make news management a top priority for a handful of trusted White House officials and cabinet secretaries who would cultivate individual reporters and news organizations; and curb the flow of information from lower levels of government. "The Reagan presidency always recognized the media as our most important single constituency," recalls Reagan pollster Richard Wirthlin. This realization led Reagan to meet periodically during his first term with small groups of reporters and columnists for off-the-record chats. He proved to be a genial companion, always ready with a funny story or a pleasant anecdote, but he rarely made any news. He preferred simply to recite well-worn lines from his speeches, or comments that his aides had scripted in advance.

Otherwise, Reagan communicated with the country directly through set-piece speeches and carefully calculated announcements by himself and his aides. More often than not, he appeared amid brilliantly conceived settings that conveyed patriotism or other large themes—visuals that the TV networks found irresistible. Among his favorites were backdrops featuring American flags, police officers and soldiers, and gorgeous scenery.

In a draft of a campaign plan for 1984, Wirthlin wrote that television was "powerful, intimate, uncontrolled, and thereby potentially damaging to an incumbent president." So Reagan and his staff resolved to control the medium as much as possible by carefully scripting his every word and deed. They succeeded brilliantly, capitalizing on Reagan's ability to hold viewers' attention and make them believe in his sincerity.

"The modern presidency is of necessity a performance—a media performance—and the modern arts of president-playing are to be celebrated, not disdained," says historian James

David Barber. "They make politics interesting and thus encourage participation. They translate complexity into simplicity, which, in real-world politics, is a prerequisite for action. At their best, they enliven and expand the national classroom where the lessons have to do with life and death. The bright side of presidential dramatics is inspiration.

"The dark side is the power of drama to overwhelm reason: the lure of illusion, the fracturing of logic, the collapse of political conversation. The dark side is the drift into the swamp of fantasy and on over the brink of disaster. Drama offers interest, but it risks political insanity. That process begins with contempt for the facts."

Reagan's respect for the facts was, at best, episodic. Despite his constant citation of statistics, he frequently got his information wrong. For example, at one of his press conferences in the spring of 1982, he repeatedly made misstatements in the most egregious way. He was wrong when he said Social Security had not been touched in his budget: The rate of growth had in fact been slowed. He was incorrect when he said programs for pregnant women had not been reduced: They had been cut by $200 million. He was in error when he said the overall poverty budget had been increased: It had not gone up at all. "Give Mr. Reagan a good script," wrote journalist James Reston, "a couple of invisible TV screens, and a half hour of prime time, and he'll convince the people they have nothing to fear but the facts." Reagan's aides argued that the country would forgive him such mistakes because voters liked his TV-enhanced leadership skills.

Reagan's background in Hollywood prepared him for the White House in ways beyond his ability to communicate on TV. In 1951 he told an awards dinner: "Certain elements of the press, the kind that are addicted to yellow journalism, certain types of gossip columnists, and so forth decided that they could attract more readers and sell more papers and get more listeners if they always went in for the more flamboyant, the more colorful, the exaggerated side of things, and in most cases the messy side of things." He complained that reporters had invaded his and other celebrities' private lives, a reference to his divorce from Jane Wyman and the sensationalistic coverage it received in the gossip columns and elsewhere. But while he had learned to distrust the press, he also tempered his dislike with a sensible recognition that it was counterproductive to cross swords constantly with the news media (a lesson that Richard Nixon, for example, never learned).

As president, Reagan came to terms with the ceaseless media scrutiny in the White House. But it was not always easy. Ronald and Nancy Reagan were always upset when reporters covered his various physical ailments in discomfiting detail. They complained angrily when the TV networks broadcast graphic depictions of his bowel when he came down with colon cancer.

One day, Deaver came into Reagan's office when he learned that the president wanted to travel secretly to Bethesda Naval Medical Center, without notifying the press, to get checked for colon cancer and prostate cancer. It was a matter of manhood with Reagan to keep such matters private. But Deaver said, "Mr. President, you know you can't do that. Sure, we could slip you into the back of a car with a hat and a raincoat on and get you out of the White House, but in fifteen minutes, word would get out and the stock market would drop, and the Soviets would go on alert."

Reagan fumed: "You want me to go into the press room, drop my pants, and show 'em my pecker!"

Deaver said that wasn't what he wanted at all—just a simple notice to the press about what was going on. Reagan quickly relented and allowed Deaver to notify reporters. As president, he knew he had become public property.

❖ ❖ ❖

". . . all that is right with, or heroized by, America."

Despite the recession and midterm election setbacks, Reagan retained a firm belief in his policies, and had stayed with them. As 1984 progressed, there was no ongoing crisis such as Carter's Iranian hostage debacle and, most important, the economy rebounded. Unemployment hovered at 7 percent and inflation only 4 percent. The massive income-tax cuts and increased defense spending finally fueled consumption spending and eventually helped create a recovery. As the November election approached, the economy reached boom levels, with relatively low inflation and plentiful jobs, despite the burgeoning deficits. Voters quickly forgot the bad times, which they attributed to Jimmy Carter, and gave Reagan credit for the good.

This was the beginning of the go-go eighties. Reagan's tax cuts benefited mainly the well-to-do, Wall Street, and to some extent the middle class, while his budget cuts made life tougher for the less fortunate. Social critics complained that the Reagan era was turning out to be one in which greed and materialism were celebrated, despite all the president's talk about family values and the benign nature of the private sector.

Politically, he used social issues to drive a wedge between the Democrats and some of their core constituencies—notably the working class and ethnic Catholics—by getting tough on

REAGAN & THE MEDIA

Reagan looked as if he knew the press corps very well, but it was a false impression. He recognized only a handful of media regulars, such as Sam Donaldson of ABC, Helen Thomas of UPI, Lou Cannon of *The Washington Post*, and a few other important and/or favorable veterans who were placed by his press secretary in prime front row seats for news conferences. Beyond that first tier, reporters who covered the White House were strangers to him, and this void caused its share of embarrassing moments.

Prior to his press conferences, which were prime-time extravaganzas staged in the ceremonial East Room, he would be briefed extensively by aides and would often take questions in the family theater in the East Wing, with staffers posing as pesky journalists. After this rehearsal, the staff would prepare a large chart that displayed each reporter's assigned seat, with his or her photo attached. A few minutes before the start of the press conference, Reagan would walk into a holding room and watch a television monitor as government camera crews panned the East Room. Press aides would point out reporters whom Reagan should call on. Then,

at the podium, Reagan would use still another seating chart, with the names of each reporter underlined or marked in yellow.

One night the staff decided that Reagan was to call on Bob Thompson, then Washington bureau chief of Hearst Newspapers. But the president was running late and didn't have a chance to preidentify Thompson on the TV monitor. When the moment came, Reagan looked down at his seating chart, looked up smoothly toward Thompson's assigned chair, and, breaking into a big grin, called on "Bob." There was no response, and other reporters began mumbling to each other in puzzlement. Was the president suffering from a mental lapse—right before their eyes?

It turned out that Bob had stayed home that night, not having been informed that he would be called on. He was sipping a glass of wine and taking notes on a yellow pad in his living room. "All of a sudden, the president called my name, and I stood up in my living room," Thompson recalled. Another reporter who was sitting in his seat ended up blurting out a question to the confused president.

Reagan also had a penchant for calling on women reporters who wore red, Nancy's favorite color. Realizing this, more and more female reporters began wearing red dresses or jackets, and the president called on them. At one point a woman journalist wore elbow-length red gloves, and Reagan allowed her a question. Soon after, a male reporter wore a bright red jacket, and Reagan called on him, too.

The prime-time press conference had become a hollow spectacle.

Sometimes being the Great Communicator meant not communicating at all. Reagan often let reporters shout questions to him while he was walking to the presidential helicopter. The roar of the rotors made it appear that nothing could be heard, but the reporters would yell and look foolish while Reagan would incline his head, cup his ear, and indicate that he couldn't hear anything—unless, of course, he heard a question that he wanted to answer.

For Reagan's handlers, it was an ideal situation: The president seemed friendly and accessible, even willing to answer questions, but that darn helicopter was just too loud.

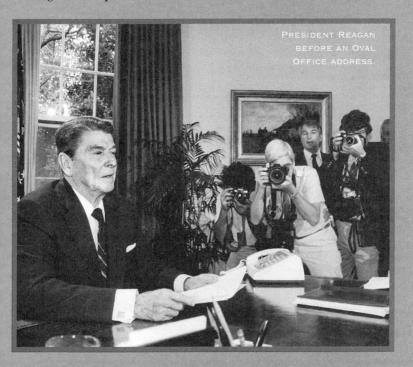

PRESIDENT REAGAN BEFORE AN OVAL OFFICE ADDRESS.

crime, opposing school busing, rejecting quotas for racial integration, and taking a stand against abortion. He also appointed many conservative judges to the federal bench.

While environmentalists opposed him strenuously, he authorized Interior secretary James Watt to open up vast tracts of public land in the West to energy development, while Environmental Protection Agency administrator Ann Burford tried to weaken standards for air pollution as an excessive burden on industry and the marketplace. Congress blocked many of these initiatives, but through them Reagan cemented his political strength among many powerful interests in the West, including industrialists and ranchers.

Still, many middle-class Americans supported him on his commonsense initiatives, such as his tough stance on crime, and the Republican Party came to dominate these "values" issues during his presidency. Just as important, Reagan never alienated political moderates. Americans were willing to tolerate their areas of disagreement with him because they liked his overall leadership and felt that at least he was candid about his views and was not dissembling or deceiving them. Consequently, he nearly made the GOP the nation's majority party.

Meanwhile, on foreign policy, the president had talked tough against the Communists, yet had maintained the peace, and not an inch of territory had been seized by what Reagan called "the evil empire." He pointed out that no longer were so-called second-rate powers, Reds, or fanatical bullies able to humiliate Uncle Sam, as they had in Vietnam, Afghanistan, and Iran. Reagan sounded his reelection theme in his State of the Union address in January 1983: "America is back, standing tall."

The goal of his campaign was to make Reagan stand for patriotism and the future, while Walter Mondale, his Democratic opponent and the former vice president under

Jimmy Carter, would stand for doubt, pessimism, and the past. Reagan strategist Stuart Spencer argued in a strategy memo that it was not enough for the president to point to his "substantive record of aging victories"; he needed to focus on his leadership, strength, and competence, and a "caring, father image that makes most Americans feel good about their president. . . . [Even] Mondale's physical characteristics work for us. He is perceived as a wimp."

As the campaign progressed into 1984, Reagan succeeded in deepening the contrast. By June, Republican strategist Richard Darman had advised Reagan in a memo to "paint Mondale as (a) weak, (b) a creature of special interests, (c) old-style, (d) unprincipled, (e) soft in his defense of freedom, patriotic values, American interests, (f) in short, [Jimmy] Carter II." Darman added that the goal should be: "Paint RR as the personification of all that is right with, or heroized by, America. Leave Mondale in a position where an attack on Reagan is tantamount to an attack on America's idealized image of itself— where a vote against Reagan is, in some subliminal sense, a vote against a mythic 'AMERICA.' "

Mondale enjoyed a brief surge of popularity after the Democratic National Convention in San Francisco that July, bringing him to within 7 percentage points of Reagan in GOP polls. But then Reagan began opening up a big lead once again with his dogged emphasis on optimism, while Mondale talked in negative terms about the country and its problems.

Mondale had also admitted that he would raise taxes if he were elected—clearing the way for Reagan to charge that he was a "tax and spend" Democrat who would dip into Americans' wallets as his first order of business, while Reagan would do so only as a last resort. Mondale's choice of New York representative Geraldine Ferraro as his vice-presidential running

Reagan and Bush at final public campaign appearance before the 1984 election.

mate initially worried Reagan's advisers as a bold stroke that could attract millions of women voters. But Ferraro ran into trouble when questions were raised about her husband's finances, and her reputation as a northeastern liberal reinforced Mondale's image as a "tax and spend liberal"; all this helped push the South and much of the West even further into the GOP corner. By late summer, Reagan was 20 points ahead.

It was not all smooth sailing for him, however. On August 11, he was preparing to deliver his weekly radio address from his Santa Barbara ranch when he started joking into an open microphone. "My fellow Americans," he said, apparently not realizing that he was being recorded, "I am pleased to tell you today that I've signed legislation that will outlaw Russia forever. We begin bombing in five minutes." The remark was a big story, and there was a brief resurrection of public concern that the president was war-happy. But Mondale failed to exploit the gaffe effectively, and most voters apparently considered it simply a tasteless attempt at humor.

Reagan gave a shaky performance in his first nationally televised debate with Mondale on October 7, but came back strong in their second encounter two weeks later, and that cemented his victory.

In November 1984 Reagan scored one of the biggest landslides in American history, capturing forty-nine states and ensuring that he could proceed with a renewed conservative mandate for another four years.

1984

CHAPTER SIX

PRESIDENT: SECOND TERM

Reagan's second term was marked by the Iran-Contra scandal, which almost shattered his presidency, and by a series of steps toward arms control and rapprochement with the Soviet Union, which ensured his place as an important player in world history.

There were other successes from Reagan's point of view, including a simplification of the income-tax system and a reduction in some federal rules and regulations. But, in a remarkable irony for a man who came into office with little understanding of foreign affairs, it was prodding the Soviet Union to reduce its nuclear arms and reform its political and economic system that represented his most important achievement.

When Reagan took office, his bellicose statements and frequent condemnations of communism had struck fear in the hearts of many Americans, who worried that he might blunder into a nuclear conflagration. His rhetoric condemning the Soviet Union as the "evil empire" and his dizzying escalation of defense spending pushed the Soviets into a panic. They boosted their own military spending, at one point investing one-third to one-half of the Soviet gross national product in defense.

In the early 1980s, Reagan had convinced the European allies to accept Pershing II and cruise missiles in Central Europe, forcing the Soviets to conclude that the existing levels of their conventional forces, tanks, and short-range missiles could not stand up to the Allies. So the Soviets countered by installing long-range missiles that could carry nuclear warheads to the United States in a further escalation of the arms race.

On March 23, 1983, Reagan had proposed the Strategic Defense Initiative—a futuristic missile-defense system, dubbed "Star Wars" by the news media—that he said could be installed in space and shoot down incoming missiles if ever they were launched against the United States. There was little scientific evidence that such a system was realistic, but Reagan was captivated by the idea and regularly told aides that he had ultimate confidence that American know-how could make the system work. He imagined that the United States would give SDI to other countries, including the Soviet Union, once it was built and usher in a nuclear-free world. The system became a huge bargaining chip in superpower relations. The United States was to spend $8 billion on developing the system between 1984 and 1987.

"Even today," former White House press secretary Marlin Fitzwater wrote in 1995, "the liberal establishment in America resents having to give Reagan credit for the strategic effect this idea had on the Soviets, who bought it hook, line, and sinker. Their economy was already sagging, and they soon saw themselves with no deterrence to SDI if it was used offensively, and no money to keep up in such an audacious arms race. Ironically, in 1995 many conservative congressional leaders wanted to revive SDI, apparently not realizing that it was primarily the Reagan bluff that made it so successful. The technology itself never materialized, at least as Reagan envisioned it.

"In the summit meetings between Reagan and Mikhail Gorbachev during their terms of office," Fitzwater added, "the ultimate objective of every meeting and arms-control negotiation was to get America to back away from SDI. As former Soviet leaders now admit, there was skepticism in Moscow about SDI, but Field Marshal [Sergei] Akhromeyev [chief of staff of the Soviet armed forces] was convinced it was real, and Gorbachev concluded that the Soviet Union could not win this arms race, if only because they couldn't afford it. . . . In retrospect, we can see the remarkable portrait of an American president who changed the world through the sheer force of an idea, one that few people believed in but in which he believed so strongly that other nations had to take it seriously. How often has that happened in our history? Wilson and the League of Nations. Kennedy and going to the moon. Not often."

Michael Beschloss, a presidential scholar and specialist on the Cold War, points out that historians will long debate whether Reagan's tough policies and mammoth defense buildup caused the collapse of communism, served as a catalyst for that collapse, or simply wasted $1 trillion to accomplish an objective that would have happened anyway.

Yet the view that Reagan's influence was decisive in forcing a historic accommodation between the superpowers, if not forcing the demise of the USSR, has been bolstered by some sources in the former USSR, including Gorbachev himself. "I think we must give Ronald Reagan his due," Gorbachev said on March 29, 1996, in an interview with *U.S. News & World Report.* "He had the foresight, wisdom, and intuition—he is a very intuitive person—to take a step forward, the same step we also had to take, and enter negotiations, a dialogue, and then partnership. I think it did not enter anyone's head, either here or in the United States, that the Soviet Union would cease to exist. That thought did not occur to anyone."

Gorbachev confirmed that Reagan's insistence on pursuing research and development of SDI pushed the USSR into arms-control deals. "It played a role in the sense that it was impermissible to take the arms race into space before dealing with it on the ground. And was it possible to take it into space? I know it was, because our research showed it was, too."

Gennady Seleznyov, chairman of the State Duma, or lower house in the Russian parliament, and a Communist, went further. Seleznyov told *U.S. News & World Report* in another interview in early 1996: "Ronald Reagan's main impact was his influence over Gorbachev. Mikhail Sergeyevich was somehow hypnotized by American policy and forgot that all American presidents from the end of [World War II] through Reagan had set the breakup of the Soviet Union as their goal, and they all very consistently pursued that goal. . . . In my view, Reagan was a strong U.S. president, a person who never gave up the goals he set, who pursued those goals with determination. . . . The mandate was clear: to hasten the hour of the Soviet Union's demise, to influence the Soviet establishment by any and all means. This was done intelligently and the goal was achieved. I say this with deep sorrow, but it's a fact."

Initially a cynic about Gorbachev's intentions, Reagan nevertheless came to believe that his counterpart in Moscow was a real reformer and that historic change was imminent.

Reagan had not met a single time with his counterparts in the Kremlin during his first term. He denied that it was because he would never listen to a tribune of the "evil empire." Rather, he said it was because three elderly and ailing Soviet leaders in succession—Leonid Brezhnev, Yuri Andropov, and Konstantin Chernenko—had died before a summit meeting could be arranged. This was true only in part; the more compelling reason was that Reagan felt that the leaders of the USSR were unwilling to compromise, and he needed to show strength and resolve before he tried to achieve a rapprochement.

Yet toward the end of his first term, in a January 16, 1984, speech that was little noticed in the United States but was broadcast live throughout Western Europe, Reagan began to sound some remarkably conciliatory notes. He said that if the Soviet government behaved itself domestically by starting to reform its oppressive system and operated with civility in international affairs, he would lower the tension level. He insisted that his goal was compromise, not confrontation, and that the American and Soviet peoples had far more in common than the political and economic systems that divided their governments. In this thought he reflected similar comments that President John F. Kennedy had made in 1963. Reagan added, "Since the dawn of the nuclear age, every American president has sought to limit and end the dangerous competition in nuclear arms. I have no higher priority than to finally realize that dream."

Reagan's domestic critics—and the Soviet press—dismissed this speech as meaningless rhetoric at the start of a reelection year. In retrospect, however, it did indicate Reagan's state of mind, even though the opportunities he spoke of would not materialize until the following year, with the ascent to power of Mikhail Gorbachev as head of the USSR.

Gorbachev, fifty-four, dynamic and full of new ideas, was

chosen general secretary of the Soviet Communist Party and leader of the Soviet Union on March 11, 1985. This changed everything. "Since Richard Nixon's first summit meeting with [Leonid] Brezhnev in Moscow in 1972, there had never been a time when a politically strong U.S. president and a physically strong Soviet general secretary had been in office at the same time," wrote journalist Don Oberdorfer. "By 1973, Nixon had been hobbled by the Watergate scandal, and he was followed by the unelected (and ultimately unelectable) Gerald Ford. By the time Jimmy Carter came to office, Brezhnev was slipping physically and mentally. He was followed by Yuri Andropov and Konstantin Chernenko, both of whom enjoyed only brief periods of tolerable health. Finally in 1985, the stars were in alignment for the first time in a long time."

❖ ❖ ❖

"We've seen what the new Russian looks like. . . ."

Reagan and Gorbachev finally scheduled their first summit meeting for November 19–21, 1985, in Geneva, when Gorbachev had been general secretary of the Soviet Communist party for eight months. It would be the first summit in six and a half years and only the eleventh since World War II.

Such summits became passé after the Cold War ended, but they were anything but routine in the 1980s. The first Reagan-Gorbachev encounter had all the earmarks of a historic event. Here was the hard-line Cold Warrior from the West against the new-style leader from the East, and no one could know what would happen when they met face-to-face.

As the date approached, Gorbachev stole a march on Reagan in world opinion by launching a series of initiatives that made him appear to be a peacemaker while Reagan remained mired in Cold War rhetoric. He proposed an indefinite freeze in building strategic offensive arms and in the research and development of space-based weapons. He stopped the deployment of Soviet intermediate-range missiles in Europe and said the deployment would be halted permanently if Washington would do the same. Reagan rejected both initiatives.

As the summit drew near, White House media adviser Deaver went to the president's residence for a chat. Deaver told Reagan, "You have taught me there is a reason for you being here. Maybe this is the reason you are here, the reason you were spared after being shot." Deaver added that no one else in government, no matter what their expertise, had the destiny of Ronald Reagan. "Why not clear them all out and just talk to Gorbachev by yourself?" Deaver suggested. "If you're the guy, you should see him yourself." Reagan agreed.

He told other aides that he would draw on his earlier experiences negotiating for the Screen Actors' Guild in Hollywood. "Negotiations would sometimes go on for days, and finally my opposite number would give a little signal," Reagan recalled. "Then we would go to the men's room for a short break. There we would make a deal without any of our aides to second-guess us." That was the simplistic formula he had for dealing with the "evil empire," and some of his advisers were extremely nervous about the outcome.

Reagan said he would not bargain away national security and he assumed Gorbachev would feel the same way. He declared that he would never allow the Soviets to achieve military superiority and would insist that any nuclear arms deals be carefully verified because the Communists would cheat if given the chance. Yet the president said he wanted peace and would do his best to ease tensions.

The leadup to the summit signaled that something important was finally changing in the USSR. For the first time since 1961, the Soviet news agency Tass requested an interview with the president, and Reagan granted it. Then, on November 9, he was allowed to make a speech on the Voice of America to the Soviet people without the Communists jamming the broadcast. Reagan's message was conciliatory: The American people wanted peace and bore no ill will toward the Soviet people.

As Reagan was traveling to Geneva on *Air Force One* on November 16, he learned that Defense secretary Caspar Weinberger, a notorious hard-liner toward Moscow, had written a letter to the president advising him to stand firm against the Soviets on arms control. The letter had been leaked to *The New York Times*, and several White House officials thought the leak was designed to torpedo the summit. News commentators criticized the administration for allowing its divisions to be aired in public almost on the eve of the meetings.

It became clear just how much the Soviet leadership had changed when the Reaganites lost the first few rounds of the head-to-head public-relations battle with Gorbachev and his aides in Geneva. The Soviets gave the world's media extraordinary access and generated a steady diet of flattering stories in the week prior to the summit, while the Americans were hardly in evidence.

In an attempt to find a bond, Reagan began the talks with Gorbachev by saying, "You and I were born in small towns about which nobody's ever heard and no one ever expected anything of either of us." Reagan also startled Gorbachev by speculating that it would be easier for them to work together "if there was a threat to this world from some other species, from another planet, outside in the universe." If that happened, the president said, "We'd forget all the little local differences that we have between our countries, and we would find out once and for all that we really are all human beings here on this earth together." Gorbachev was not impressed; he thought Reagan was raising an extraneous, bizarre issue in order to divert attention from the matters at hand.

The president explained his intentions to his staff after the first morning meeting: At an appropriate moment, he would ask Gorbachev to chat in private. That afternoon, at the poolhouse of the Château Fleur D'Eau overlooking Lake Geneva, Reagan and Gorbachev held their initial one-on-one from 3:55 to 4:44 P.M. They talked as Deaver had suggested, while sitting in easy chairs before a fire in a poolhouse with a panoramic view of Lake Geneva, dubbed by White House press secretary Larry Speakes "the fireside summit."

After relating how Gorbachev complained about the evils of capitalism and cast doubt on U.S. intentions, Reagan had to calm his frustrated aides. "I can't believe a man as savvy as Gorbachev is using those terms," he said. "I suspect he really believes what he's saying. Maybe we can educate him otherwise when he comes to see us [in the United States]."

Reagan also reported to aides that Gorbachev said he had the Bible read to him as a child by his Christian grandmother. And while Reagan didn't ask for more information after this revelation, he came away persuaded that Gorbachev had religious feelings that might make him easier to deal with. Deaver told me later that Reagan became convinced that Gorbachev believed in a "higher power," reinforcing the president's instinct that this Soviet leader was capable of compromise.

There turned out to be few concrete accomplishments in Geneva, both at the private sessions between the two leaders and in larger meetings involving senior U.S. and Soviet officials. They remained at loggerheads on many specific policy questions, especially Reagan's insistence on building the Strategic Defense Initiative. But Reagan was heartened nonetheless. The two leaders agreed to accelerate the pace of arms-control talks and meet again. More important, Reagan said he came away convinced that Gorbachev was sincere about wanting a nuclear-reduction agreement. As he flew home on *Air Force One*, the president told his staff: "We've seen what the new Russian looks like. Now maybe we can figure out how to deal with him."

A few days later, Reagan reminisced about the fifteen hours he had spent with the Soviet leader and offered his impressions of the man. "We sat in a room and I told him, 'Here we are, between us we could decide things that could probably bring peace for years and generations to come. And if we could erase these things that have made us suspicious of each other, it would be very worthwhile.' . . . I think I'm some judge of acting, and I don't think Gorbachev was acting. He, I believe, is sincere, as we are, in wanting an agreement, but he feels we have no right to lecture him about human rights in the Soviet Union; he sincerely believes that human rights are being violated in our country as well." Again, his tolerance of the Soviet leader surprised and troubled many White House aides, especially the hawks.

By the following year, Reagan had become so entranced with Gorbachev that he tried to engineer one of the biggest and perhaps most dangerous foreign policy surprises in recent history.

When the two men met on October 11–12, 1986, in Reykjavik, Iceland, the talks started off with great promise. Gorbachev seemed willing to eliminate all medium-range nuclear missiles from Europe. He also seemed willing to accept Reagan's proposal that all offensive missiles belonging to the United States and the Soviets should be eliminated over the next ten years. By the afternoon of Sunday, October 12, with the talks well into overtime, Reagan suddenly said he would be willing to eliminate all U.S. nuclear weapons—missiles, bombs, everything—if the Soviets did the same. That, Reagan's own experts agreed, would have been a massive error that would have made the West vulnerable to Moscow's huge advantage in conventional forces. (Secretary of State George Shultz, sitting next to Reagan, remained silent, apparently too exhausted to warn his boss away.) But when Gorbachev insisted that Reagan abandon the Strategic Defense Initiative, the president balked. He was unwilling to give up the project and argued that, even though many U.S. scientists considered it technologically unfeasible, he had faith that it would provide an invaluable shield against nuclear attack. Gorbachev saw it as an escalation of the arms race. The summit broke down.

When the two men walked out of Hofdi House, where the talks had been held, the president seemed shocked that their efforts had failed.

"I'm sorry it didn't work out," Gorbachev said as he approached his limousine in the biting cold.

"It could have worked out if you had wanted it to," Reagan replied icily.

Reagan's ignorance of the issues sometimes dismayed not only his staff but also the president himself. After meeting with Gorbachev at the White House on December 9, 1987, he was upset with how he could not keep up with the Soviet leader's command of facts and figures. After a break in the talks, Reagan looked uncharacteristically glum and told Howard Baker, his chief of staff at the time: "I better go home and do my home-

Ronald Reagan with Mikhail Gorbachev in Washington, D.C., December 8, 1987.

work. Mikhail has all those details." But Baker replied, "No, you go home and relax. All you have to remember is that no matter what he says, you're the president of the United States." Reagan brightened. "I guess you're right. See you tonight." He went to the White House residence for some private time before the evening's state dinner; when he reappeared, his confidence was back. Such periods of self-doubt were rare because Reagan thought his principles were enough to carry the day; aides were the ones who could come up with the details.

The next day, December 10, Reagan was again his old self. During a delay before the two leaders agreed on a final communiqué, he stunned everyone, including Gorbachev, by relating a story he had read in *People* about a twelve-hundred-pound man who was unable to leave his bedroom. "This is a real man," Reagan said sincerely. "He went to the bathroom one day, and he fell in the doorway and got stuck. It frightened him so much to get stuck that he went on a diet."

Vice President George Bush, Treasury Secretary James Baker, and Anatoly Dobrynin, Soviet ambassador to the United States, were nonplused. For his part, Gorbachev asked through his interpreter, "Is this real fact?"

"Yes," Reagan assured him. "Since his diet, his knee measurement shrank to one and one-third meters around. When the diet is complete, he wants to visit the grave of his mother."

Gorbachev left the president, saying he wanted to find a men's room. But White House press secretary Marlin Fitzwater spotted the Soviet leader in a hallway, "gesturing wildly to Dobrynin, no doubt asking what in the hell this twelve-hundred-pound man was all about." No one knew but Reagan, and that's the last he said of the matter to Gorbachev.

Prior to the December 1987 summit, aides were briefing Reagan about the slow pace of change in the Soviet Union's hard-line policies when the president brought them up short. "I know Gorbachev wants to change that," Reagan said. "I'm sure sometimes the bureaucrats in the Kremlin don't tell him things. Let's give him the benefit of the doubt."

His hard-line staffers looked at each other incredulously. What happened to the zealous anti-Communist Ronald Reagan? But his optimistic instinct was right. Reagan was correct in his fundamental assessment that communism was crumbling from within, hastened by massive financial, diplomatic, and military pressure by the United States.

At that December summit in Washington, Reagan and

Gorbachev finally did sign an agreement eliminating intermediate-range nuclear weapons. That was only the beginning. Within the next three years, the USSR would allow German reunification, give up its satellite countries, and break up as a Communist state. Reagan's staunch anti-communism and his policy of putting great pressure on the "evil empire" had apparently paid big dividends.

Another one of Reagan's pet ideas later came to fruition under Bush. On his *Marine One* helicopter en route to Andrews Air Force Base, Reagan would look out the window and point out various sights to aides. "Look at that," he would say, peering down at cars in the suburban driveways and at occasional swimming pools in the backyards. "I really wish Gorbachev could see that." To Reagan, these were symbols of middle-class prosperity and testaments to the American Dream that could only impress the Soviet leader. Reagan never got to show Gorbachev the sights, but Bush did, and the Soviet leader was indeed impressed, just as Reagan said he would be.

◈ ◈ ◈

"I didn't have cancer."

One of Reagan's most serious problems throughout his presidency was his health. As with many people in their seventies, his hearing deteriorated markedly, sometimes making him appear befuddled when he could not clearly hear conversations around him or questions posed to him.

Far worse, in July 1985 he was diagnosed with a malignant tumor in his colon; doctors removed the growth along with two feet of his bowel, and he recovered quickly, as he had done after the assassination attempt.

And Reagan's optimism remained undiminished. When a reporter asked him how he dealt with cancer, Reagan said, "I didn't have cancer. I had something inside of me that had cancer in it, and it was removed." This, of course, was self-delusion, but it helped Reagan come to terms with his illness.

The White House made Reagan's recovery look normal, releasing information that put him in the most favorable light and making sure that all photographs showed him as hale and hearty as possible. "The first photograph of the president after surgery," boasted former White House press secretary Larry Speakes, "was artfully arranged to conceal the nasogastric tube that had been inserted in Reagan's nose and was held in place by tape. The photo showed Mrs. Reagan leaning over to kiss her husband. Her face strategically covered the tube."

He was back at the White House on July 20, a week after his surgery.

Ten days later, doctors found a malignancy on the right side of his nose and removed it. In October 1985 and July 1987 he would have two more skin cancers removed from his nose, again with no detriment to his overall health.

❧ ❧ ❧

"I made a very deliberate decision . . . "

The administration's fortunes began to deteriorate in the fall of 1986. On October 5 a small plane piloted by a middle-aged American named Eugene Hasenfus was shot down over the steamy jungles of Nicaragua. He was quickly captured by the country's Marxist regime, which discovered that his cargo con-

TROUBLE BEHIND
THE FACADE

Reagan's relationship with his four children was often strained, sometimes embarrassingly so. For example, he did not attend the wedding of his younger son, Ron, in New York, in 1980. Nor did he attend the wedding of his elder daughter, Maureen, in California in 1981. Reagan rarely saw his only grandson, Cameron, the child of his adopted son Michael, during the first few years of the boy's life in the 1970s and early 1980s. And he rarely saw Michael's daughter, Ashley, after her birth in 1982.

All in all, it was far from the Norman Rockwell portrait that Reagan idealized in his public rhetoric.

Michael, whom Reagan and Wyman had adopted in March 1945, was perhaps the most embittered about the situation. After Reagan and Wyman divorced, the future president did not have sustained contact with young Michael except on weekends. In his 1988 autobiography *On the Outside Looking In*, Michael, a businessman and powerboat racer, revealed that a camp counselor had molested him and taken nude photos when he was seven years old.

In May 1981, Michael wrote a business letter to officials at Tinker Air Force Base in Oklahoma attempting to put his company, Dana Ingalls Profile, Inc., of Burbank, California, an aircraft parts manufacturer, on an approved list of suppliers. The letter said, "I know that with my father's leadership at the White House, this country's armed services are going to be rebuilt and strengthened." Michael was severely criticized in the news media for trading on the family name, and the resulting controversy caused him to resign his job. Nancy Reagan made matters worse when she said Michael had blundered.

After continued sniping by Michael at his father and stepmother, the family feud widened. In November 1984 Maureen, the president's daughter by Wyman, said Michael was the one at fault because he had declared "war" on Nancy.

Not that Maureen was reluctant to break with her dad in public. For example, she supported abortion rights and the Equal Rights Amendment to the Constitution, two positions he abhorred. But she remained loyal to the Republican Party and served the Republican National Com-

LEFT TO RIGHT, PATTI DAVIS, FIANCÉ PAUL GRILLEY, NANCY AND RONALD REAGAN, DORIA REAGAN, AND RON JR., CHRISTMAS 1983.

mittee as special adviser on women's issues. Maureen also campaigned aggressively for her father's reelection as president.

Another series of embarrassments was caused by Patti Davis, the elder child of Nancy and Ronald Reagan, who used her mother's maiden name. In her 1986 semi-autobiographical novel *Home Front*, Patti, an actress and author, described a father as a distant figure who gave little emotional support to his family.

On policy issues she differed with her parents on nuclear power, abortion, marijuana, the Vietnam War, and premarital sex, and complained that for much of her life she was inhibited from speaking out for fear it would hurt her father's political career. But she overcame such trepidations and began to appear at antinuclear rallies. Patti lived for a year with a rock-and-roll guitarist and posed for the July 1994 *Playboy.*

Ron, the youngest sibling, was a ballet dancer who became a contributing editor of *Playboy* and sometime television performer. A Yale dropout, he lived with a former dance school classmate, Doria Palmieri, whom he later married. In October 1982 he drew temporary unemployment from the government after he was furloughed from the Joffrey ballett company in New York.

He admitted trading on the family name to gain attention for his show-business career but said he refused to engage in "trashing my folks in a mean way." His fame soared when he appeared on NBC's "Saturday Night Live" in February 1986 and did a takeoff on the film *Risky Business.* In the skit, Ron danced raucously in a simulated White House while his parents were away at Camp David.

As Ronald Reagan went into decline from Alzheimer's disease, many of the rifts were healed, and the family seemed closer than ever. The former president now greatly enjoys the company of his children and grandchildren.

sisted of a variety of weapons intended for the anti-government Contra rebels. The Nicaraguan leaders branded the flight a CIA covert operation, and the White House reflexively denied it. But under questioning, Hasenfus told his captors that the Reagan administration was indeed behind the gun-running, in direct violation of the Boland Amendments, laws passed by Congress in 1982 and 1984 that prohibited attempts to overthrow the regime in Managua and any secret efforts to arm the Contras.

Then in November, a Lebanese newspaper disclosed that Robert McFarlane, the president's chief national security adviser, had conducted secret talks with the Iranian government of Ayatollah Khomeini in an effort to trade arms for hostages. This came despite President Reagan's repeated assurances to the American people that he would never make deals with terrorist governments. The administration at first tried to dismiss the Lebanese report. Later, administration officials argued that their goal was to court "moderates" in Iran who might help win release of hostages held by pro-Iranian terrorists in Lebanon.

Then came the most dramatic revelation of all. It turned out that the profits gained from the arms sales to Iran were being used illegally to arm the Contras, half a world away in Nicaragua. Attorney General Ed Meese revealed that choice morsel of scandal in a press conference on November 25, 1986, setting off an immediate furor.

In the space of fewer than two months, the Reagan administration had been turned on its ear—accused of lawbreaking, lying, ineptitude, and deception.

The president's loyalists attempted to blame the scandal on overzealous activism by underlings, especially Lieutenant Colonel Oliver North, a covert operator on the National Security Council staff. North admitted a variety of illegal actions, including the shredding of documents to protect the president and others in the administration. Admiral John Poindexter, who succeeded McFarlane as national security adviser, also admitted destroying records to avoid embarrassing the president. Later, North said he believed that Reagan knew about and endorsed his illegal actions. But Poindexter, North's boss, denied that Reagan knew.

In fact, one of the most dramatic developments of the Iran-Contra affair was Poindexter's testimony before Congress that he had personally authorized the use of profits from the Iranian sales to help the Contras—and had not told Reagan. "I made a very deliberate decision not to ask the president so that I could insulate him from the decision and provide some future deniability," Poindexter declared. "The buck stops here with me."

An investigatory panel chaired by former senator John Tower, a Texas Republican, found that the NSC's "rogue staff" was to blame for the fiasco, along with Reagan's inattention to detail and inept style of management.

But a separate congressional investigation controlled by Democrats concluded late in 1987 that it was Reagan who was at fault because his subordinates were following his policies "to sell arms secretly to Iran and to maintain the 'body and soul' of the Contras." Yet the committee members, acknowledging Reagan's personal popularity and the fact that he would automatically leave office little more than a year later, in January 1989, wanted to spare the nation another wrenching constitutional crisis similar to Watergate, so they did not pursue impeachment.

Finally came the investigation of special prosecutor Lawrence Walsh, a Republican and former government litigator. His report concluded that the policies that produced Iran-

Ronald Reagan, with Senators Edmund Muskie and John Tower, at the release of the Tower Commission Report, February 1987.

Contra were developed at the "highest levels" of the Reagan administration and that many senior officials had lied to cover up their complicity and the president's knowledge.

Walsh filed criminal charges against fourteen individuals, including Poindexter and North, who were convicted of various charges, only to have their convictions overturned largely because their testimony before congressional committees was inadmissible in their criminal trials (Congress had granted them immunity from criminal prosecution). McFarlane pleaded guilty to withholding information and lying to Congress but received a light sentence. President George Bush would pardon former Defense secretary Weinberger in late 1992 after Weinberger was scheduled to be tried for perjury.

"There was no order in the place."

The scandal left Reagan's credibility temporarily in tatters. He had escaped the worst opprobrium, but most of his critics argued that, at the very least, he had demonstrated startling incompetence and a willingness to look the other way when things got messy.

For his part, Reagan insisted that he did not initially approve arms sales to Iran specifically to win release of any hostages—that, he claimed, happened by accident—and he denied that he knew of the diversion of funds to the Contras.

The worst part of Iran-Contra, however, was the erosion it caused in public confidence in government—and in the president himself.

Reagan knew he needed to get beyond the scandal, and he used a prime-time press conference in the ceremonial East Room on March 19, 1987, to do just that. He prepared for it laboriously. Press secretary Marlin Fitzwater and his staff had prepared forty-three Iran-Contra questions that reporters might ask. Fearing that the journalists would try to trip Reagan up by demonstrating his ignorance on other topics, the staff gave him twenty more pages of single-spaced talking points on not only Iran-Contra but also a wide range of foreign and domestic issues and the economy. Still another twenty-five-page report was sent to the president, summarizing the controversy by adviser David Abshire. Reagan was also rehearsed for two two-hour sessions in the White House's family theater.

Reagan's aides realized that he would never come to believe he traded arms for hostages, which he said he would never do. Instead, he believed that someone in his administration had committed the deed, but he never admitted that he had approved such a thing. It had been done without his knowledge, he said, by underlings such as North and Poindexter.

". . . Reagan's great strength as a president was that he knew himself and what he believed," Fitzwater explained. ". . . Good people would do the right thing. Above all, Ronald Reagan believed he was a good person. This belief was at the core of his political principles—that conservatism was good for America, and American was a good, hardworking, ethical nation that should be a role model to the world. Iran-Contra shook those beliefs in Ronald Reagan for the simple reason that it made people doubt his word."

Reagan gave a bravura performance at the press conference. He did not provide any new information, but seemed sincere in denying any wrongdoing on his own part and arguing that he told the country and the Congress what he knew about the episode as soon as it was revealed to him by aides. Before long, Americans lost interest in the Iran-Contra affair as the economy boomed, relations with the Soviets improved, and national confidence returned. Reagan's popularity, which had dropped precipitously, rebounded as well.

The Iran-Contra revelations showed, however, that Ronald Reagan, who turned seventy-six in February 1987, was no longer the political force he used to be. The administration's domestic agenda seemed paralyzed, and the White House was losing its once-deft political touch. When the Dow Jones Industrial Average dropped a record 508 points on October 19, 1987, Reagan's response seemed Herbert Hoover-like. He said the economy remained sound and the market was simply engaging in a natural correction; this may have been true (the economy continued to grow at a solid pace for the next three years), but he left the impression of a man who lacked the energy and ideas to avert a crisis.

Reagan, increasingly a lame duck, suffered a deep disappointment when he lost a nomination fight to confirm conservative Judge Robert Bork to the U.S. Supreme Court in 1987. Bork was abrasive and arrogant, and he alienated many members of the Democrat-controlled Senate during his confirmation hearings before the Senate Judiciary Committee. But equally important in his downfall were the institutional mistakes of the White House. For one thing, Bork may have been simply too conservative to win confirmation without an early and aggressive campaign on his behalf, and the White House did not realize that until it was too late. For another, Joseph Biden, chairman of the Judiciary Committee, was running for president and was not about to give the White House an easy victory. Further, Reagan's popularity was being undermined by the Iran-Contra scandal. After a struggle lasting three and a half months, the Senate rejected Bork 58 to 42, an overwhelming repudiation of an administration that seemed adrift.

In the winter of 1987, when former senator Howard Baker was preparing to take over as White House chief of staff after the firing of the abrasive Donald Regan, there were many rumors in the press corps that the president was dangerously disengaged. He seemed more forgetful than usual, Regan's aides said, and was not on top of his job. Baker heard the talk, and he dispatched James Cannon, a close friend and trusted adviser, to find out the truth. If things were serious enough, if the president was "unable to discharge the powers and duties of his office," the Twenty-fifth Amendment provided that the vice president should take over.

THE IMPORTANCE OF
BEING NANCY

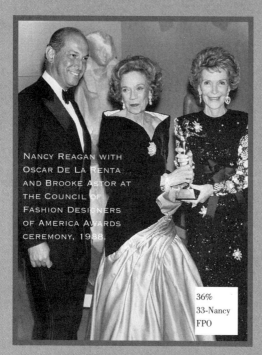

NANCY REAGAN WITH
OSCAR DE LA RENTA
AND BROOKE ASTOR AT
THE COUNCIL OF
FASHION DESIGNERS
OF AMERICA AWARDS
CEREMONY, 1988.

36%
33-Nancy
FPO

In the White House, Nancy Reagan created a safe haven and comfort zone for Ronald Reagan that he found indispensable. But she came to symbolize a devotion to luxury that many Americans considered excessive, especially while millions of citizens were suffering from the recession. Nancy loved to wear expensive gowns by designers Galanos and Adolfo and, along with her husband, enjoyed socializing at fancy parties with millionaire California friends including the Alfred Bloomingdales, the Justin Darts, and the Earle Jorgensens. And she refused to give up her lavish lifestyle, saying that Americans expected the president and First Lady to demonstrate a certain degree of taste and class.

Mrs. Reagan always insisted that she was not her husband's puppetmaster, but on occasion she seemed to be just that. On August 1, 1984, during a photo opportunity at his Santa Barbara ranch, the president was asked what he could do to bring the Soviets to the bargaining table on nuclear arms reductions and other issues. Reagan thought for several seconds, looking at his feet and bobbing his head in silence, apparently unsure how to respond. Microphones caught Mrs. Reagan whispering to him: "Doing everything we can."

The president broke into a big

smile and said, "Doing everything we can." That moment struck many critics of the Reagans as a paradigm of their relationship, and indicative of the president's disengagement from the details of his own policies.

Using private donations, largely from wealthy friends and admirers, she redecorated the White House residence and bought a 220-place set of china emblazoned with the presidential seal for more than $200,000. Many Americans were shocked that she was so interested in dishware at a time of great economic dislocation. If anything, Mrs. Reagan's image was worse than her husband's, especially at the beginning of their White House years. She endured severe criticism for seeming too interested in wealth and glamor and, later, for insisting that some events on her husband's schedule be guided by astrological charts. She admitted she was influenced by the stars, but said it was a natural reaction to her fear that her husband might be the victim of a second assassination attempt or catastrophic accident.

She did take steps periodically to improve her image. One such occasion was the Washington Gridiron dinner of 1982, a white-tie affair for six hundred of Washington's most powerful media and political figures. Mrs. Reagan decided to puncture her image by performing a parody of an old-time Broadway tune,

"Secondhand Rose." She called it "Secondhand Clothes," and she sang it dressed in a hand-me-down costume, taking the crowd and her husband by surprise. Her lyrics:

I'm wearing secondhand
clothes
Secondhand clothes
They're quite the style
In the spring fashion shows.
Even my new trench coat with
fur collar
Ronnie bought for ten cents
on the dollar.

Secondhand gowns
And old hand-me-downs
The china is the only thing
that's new.
Even though they tell me that
I'm no longer queen,
Did Ronnie have to buy me
that new sewing machine?
Secondhand clothes, second-
hand clothes,
I sure hope Ed Meese sews.

She got a standing ovation. Official Washington, especially the press, likes nothing so much as self-deprecation in public figures, and Nancy Reagan had given it to them. Her press reviews were never quite so biting again. Her commitment to a "Just Say No" antidrug campaign also improved her public standing.

After spending the better part of two days talking with various White House officials, especially aides to the ousted Regan, Cannon concluded that there was indeed cause for concern. "Chaos," Cannon recalled. "There was no order in the place. The staff system had just broken down. It had just evaporated. There was no pattern of analysis, no coming together." As for Reagan, the interviews with staffers revealed several serious problems, Cannon said: "They told stories about how inattentive and inept the president was. He was lazy; he wasn't interested in the job. They said he wouldn't read the papers they gave him—even short position papers and documents. They said he wouldn't come over to work—all he wanted to do was to watch movies and television at the residence." Cannon recommended privately to Baker that he consider the possibility of applying the Twenty-fifth Amendment.

The next morning, Monday, March 2, Baker, Cannon, and two other Baker confidants, Thomas Griscom and A. B. Culvahouse, attended meetings with Reagan and watched him closely. They concluded that he was doing just fine, and that the White House aides with the horror stories were exaggerating; they were largely supporters of Donald Regan who were embittered that their boss had been fired. Regan, it turned out, was furious at both the president and Nancy Reagan. He told associates that Nancy had persuaded her husband to get rid of him, and he could not forgive them for it.

Throughout 1987 and 1988, in fact, Nancy Reagan was a more important and assertive figure than ever, anxious as always to protect her husband from his frailties and from staffers she felt were not serving him well. Regan, it turned out, was one of them. She was never comfortable with his macho ways and his dismissive manner. "They had argued over the president's scheduling and his appearances," said

Fitzwater. "Regan was frustrated by the role of Mrs. Reagan's astrologer in selecting the timing of meetings and press conferences. Their phone conversations became abrupt, punctuated by long silences."

Nancy and Ronald Reagan remained soulmates of the most intense kind. She would gaze at him with such utter affection and intensity that friends and associates called it simply "The Look." And he would return her affection in equal measure.

During the superpower summit in December 1987, their partnership was particularly clear as they prepared to meet with Mikhail and Raisa Gorbachev at the White House. "They did not like to work separately on these occasions," recalled Fitzwater. "They preferred to work as a team. The president and Mrs. Reagan were always in their own world, always attached by an invisible string, always aware of each other's presence, even if both were working a handshake line or visiting at a reception. . . . This was the big game and she knew it. Her eyes never strayed from his, the actress in her was coming to the fore. She was oblivious to all around her, and the room was filling rapidly. Then she took his scarf in both hands and pulled his face close to hers, nose to nose, for a private pep talk."

It was Mrs. Reagan, of course, who won her confrontation with Donald Regan, as she always won such contests. But her role in ousting the chief of staff by turning her husband against him showed how much Ronald Reagan leaned on her during his last two years in office.

Former aides told reporters that he had clearly lost some of his mental sharpness during the final years of his presidency, 1987 and 1988. Briefers said that on occasion he forgot names of key staffers as well as important policy details. But his talented staff made up for his lapses, and he was able to rise to the occasion when the situation warranted.

"... you were terrific."

By the end of his presidency, Reagan, by this time nearly seventy-eight, was largely a ceremonial figure. He delegated ever more decisions to his staff, spent more time at Camp David and his Santa Barbara ranch, and except for stumping in California, took only a little part in campaigning for Vice President George Bush in the fall of 1988.

And after Bush won, Reagan played almost no role in the new administration, shunning even a position as informal adviser to his political heir. Friends at first said he was too worn out and wanted to pass the torch to another generation after many years of public service. But it turned out that there was another reason for his lack of interest.

In 1994 the Reagan family announced that he had been suffering from Alzheimer's disease, the crippling affliction that robs people of their memory and, eventually, most of their mental functions. It was not known how long Reagan had been afflicted with the disease, and whether it had affected his final months or years in the White House. But it was clear that the former president was not himself for some time before the announcement. For example, before his speech to the Republican National Convention in 1992, a senior adviser in his administration had come up to him backstage and found him "befuddled." Never good at remembering names, Reagan did not recognize his former aide, who hurriedly reintroduced himself to avoid embarrassment. Minutes later, Reagan managed to deliver a stirring speech to the delegates. "But afterward," the former aide recalled, "he was drained" and seemed once again confused. Reagan's years of personal involvement in American politics had come to an end.

As he approached his mid-eighties, he lived comfortably and very privately with Nancy in Bel Air, rarely making public appearances. Nancy Reagan, always his protector, became even more so now, keeping her husband away from the media to protect the heroic image crafted throughout his presidency. During one visit by a member of his White House team, the former aide mentioned that he loved Reagan's performance in a particular film, and Reagan said, "I wasn't in that movie."

The guest said, "Yes, you were, Mr. President, and you were terrific."

Reagan got up, went to a bookshelf, and looked up the title in an encyclopedia of cinema. "You're right," Reagan said, shaking his head sadly at his lapse. "I was in that movie."

As his mind deteriorated, the former president would sometimes become anxious when he was alone, a classic symptom of Alzheimer's disease. When he was up to it, he visited his office in Los Angeles to receive old friends. Sometimes he played golf to get some exercise. But his doctors advised him against horseback riding, a pastime which he had loved all his life, because he could now easily hurt himself. With Reagan unable to enjoy his beloved Rancho del Cielo in the Santa Ynez Mountains north of Santa Barbara, Nancy finally decided in the summer of 1996 to put the property up for sale. There were increasingly long periods during which he could not remember important events in his life.

Nancy confided to friends what troubled her most: Her husband had been robbed of the trait that had endeared him to so many, his sunny disposition. But she took comfort in the fact that his fellow citizens would never forget the Reagan era and the man who so optimistically presided over it.

1989

CHAPTER SEVEN

REAGAN'S LEGACY

What is Ronald Reagan's place in history?

His most dramatic initiative was his willingness to neglect domestic problems and spend extraordinary sums of money on defense to break the back of communism. Reagan and his supporters argue that the outcome was worth the cost. They contend that he put so much financial, diplomatic, and military pressure on Moscow that the USSR was forced to accept far-reaching arms-control agreements that made the world safer from nuclear war. In the end, Reagan proponents say, his policies caused the total collapse of communism and the disbanding of the Soviet Union.

Reagan's critics argue that the Soviet Union would have collapsed even if Jimmy Carter had remained president because the Communist system was rotting from within. Under this theory, Reagan wasted billions of dollars and saddled Americans with a vast debt that has debilitated the U.S. economy and kept the federal government from spending on needed social programs.

Historians will argue these matters for generations. What is indisputable, however, is that Reagan gave Americans a new sense of possibility and optimism. He showed that leadership still could make a difference in the world, and his upbeat style fundamentally reshaped his times. He considered himself an ordinary man with some extraordinary skills, a simple citizen who represented the dreams, ideals, and aspirations of the country. This is precisely what most Americans wanted their president to be, and Reagan played this, his best and most important role, extremely well.

His soaring conception of America remained constant throughout his long public career, and he delivered what was essentially the same signature speech from the 1960s with equal conviction thirty years later. The strength of his political message never changed once he embarked on his conservative crusade. "You and I have a rendezvous with destiny," he said. "We can preserve for our children this—the last, best hope of man on earth—or we can sentence them to take the first step into a thousand years of darkness. If we fail, at least let our children and our children's children say of us we justified our brief moment here. We did all that could be done."

Nancy Reagan, who knew him best, wrote in 1989:

"Ronnie didn't seek the presidency in order to become somebody; he already was somebody. And he came into office with a clear idea of what he wanted to accomplish.

"Maybe that's why he didn't seem to age in office. A president grows old when he's constantly forced to react to events, without a broad plan or an overall philosophy. Whenever something happens, he has to ask himself: My God, what am I going to do about this? Where do I stand?

Ronald Reagan on his California ranch.

"Ronnie knew exactly what he wanted to achieve in the Oval Office. His goals had been honed over a twenty-year period, and people knew exactly where he stood. Economic recovery. Greater economic freedom. A stronger defense. Less government. Those were his top priorities, and other things had to wait. He understood that if you try to accomplish everything, you run the risk of achieving nothing."

On domestic issues, some of Reagan's senior aides, especially White House chief of staff James Baker and Nancy Reagan, tried to make him seem more moderate than he was. But his conservative instincts would always return.

In 1983, ignoring the advice of his more pragmatic advisers, Reagan wrote a small book explaining his opposition to abortion, and the volume was widely distibuted in pro-life circles. Even late in his second term, when other ideologues had left his administration or tired of the fight, Reagan could be prodded into action. Every Monday, he would have lunch with senior advisers and discuss their issue papers, which had been submitted the previous Friday and reviewed by the chief of staff. The moderates were unhappy when Gary Bauer, a tireless conservative ideologue who was serving as White House domestic policy adviser, kept presenting right-of-center suggestions for the president's consideration. "Time and time again, there was an attempt to deep-six them," Bauer recalls. "They said, 'We can't waste the president's time on this.'" But Bauer knew how to capture Reagan's attention with up-close-and-personal stories.

Once he told of a girl in a southern state who was forbidden from giving her valedictory address at her high school commencement because she wanted to mention God. Reagan grew upset and said: Let's get a letter to her. "The only time he got animated was when someone brought up these incidents of Americana," Bauer said. "I would look around the table and I'd see eyes rolling and people squirming in their seats." But the president was transfixed.

Throughout 1987–88, Bauer would appear on the conservative radio and television shows of religious broadcasters, and found he could generate thousands of letters to Congress and the White House with a few well-chosen remarks. Once, he told *The Washington Post* he was looking for ways for Reagan to undertake some conservative initiatives unilaterally, without the approval of the Democratic majority in Congress, even though his second term was winding down. The day the *Post* published those quotes, Bauer was sitting in a restaurant when a call came in from the White House. An aide warned him that the First Lady was furious and wanted him to stop talking in such a provocative manner. But it turned out that Bauer had told the president of his intentions, and Reagan had approved. So Bauer said, "Sorry, the President said to do it, and I will continue unless he tells me to stop." At Nancy Reagan's behest, Bauer was never invited to a state dinner in his two years at the White House, but Reagan continued to accept his suggestions.

By maintaining his conservative base in a nonthreatening way, Reagan was able to make conservatism into a governing ideology, not just a periodic respite from liberal policies. In the process, Reagan rejuvenated the GOP. Frank Donatelli, White House political director during Reagan's second term, called Reagan "the father of the modern Republican Party."

"Ronald Reagan was the touchstone for Republicans the way Franklin Roosevelt was for Democrats," Donatelli said. "He was a rare guy in Washington. You could disagree with him but you could like him, too. Conservatives often seem too negative. Reagan didn't, and people responded to that. Even though the public had misgivings about some of his policies, they always gave him credit for having principles and trying to implement them."

As political scientist Bruce Miroff has written, "The Reagan presidency was a triumph of spectacle. In the realm of sub-

REDISCOVERING
REAGAN

THE OPENING CEREMONY OF THE RONALD REAGAN
PRESIDENTIAL LIBRARY, 1991.

In the years immediately following his presidency, political scientists, economists, and politicians gave poor grades to Ronald Reagan, largely because of the trillion-dollar national debt that he and his successor George Bush left behind. Reagan-era deficit spending crippled the federal government's ability to create new social programs, which some Democrats believed was Reagan's intention all along, and hampered the country's long-term economic growth, which was an unintended consequence of his policy.

These problems still tarnish Reagan's reputation, but his achievements began to take on more luster in the mid-nineties. Not only did Reagan receive more credit for helping to end the Cold War and vanquish communism, his impact on America's self-esteem was increasingly seen as a lasting legacy, one that politicians of all stripes began to celebrate. He showed that presidential leadership was still possible in a complex, unpredictable world, and that charisma still counted.

The rediscovering of Ronald Reagan came to full force in the 1996 presidential campaign, especially among Republicans. "All the presidential candidates in 1996 were reaching for his coattails," said Frank Donatelli, who served as Reagan's White House political director at the end of his second term. Millionaire publisher Steve Forbes promoted Reagan-style optimism and supply-side economics, arguing that tax cuts would unleash America's creative forces. Senator Phil Gramm of Texas said he had sponsored Reagan's tax cuts in Congress and was the Gipper's economic heir. Conservative commentator Patrick Bu-chanan reminded voters that he had been Reagan's White House communications director and could inspire the country to turn even more dramatically to the right. Former Tennessee governor Lamar Alexander said he wanted to devolve power to the states and localities as Reagan did. Former Senate majority leader Bob Dole of Kansas, the eventual GOP nominee, promised bluntly that he would try to be another Reagan in all respects if that was what the voters wanted.

Reagan's policies echoed through the Republican-controlled Congress of the mid- and late nineties. His long-sought goal of a line-item veto was finally enacted and endorsed by President Bill Clinton, and his dream of a balanced budget became Washington dogma after the Soviet empire disintegrated and America's massive defense buildup was no longer deemed necessary. His objective of shifting power from Washington to the states and municipalities became commonly accepted in the capital.

"Ronald Reagan is the touchstone for Republicans the way Franklin Roosevelt was for the Democrats," Donatelli said.

Even President Clinton, a Democrat, rediscovered "The Great Communicator." He modeled his reelection campaign on Reagan's successful 1984 effort, focusing on optimism and looking to a sunny future, just the way Reagan did.

stantive policy, it was marked by striking failures as well as significant successes. But even the most egregious of these failures—public exposure of the disastrous covert policy of selling arms to Iran and diverting some of the profits from the sales to the Nicaraguan Contras—proved to be only a temporary blow to the political fortunes of the most spectacular president in decades. . . . Reagan presented to his audience a multifaceted character, funny yet powerful, ordinary yet heroic, individual yet representative. He was a character richer even than Kennedy in mythic resonance."

Many economists argue that while Reagan's economic record was, on balance, negative because of the deficits he allowed to

Reagan boards Marine One for the final time as he leaves the White House on the last day of his presidency, 1989.

burgeon, his impulse to reduce taxes was healthy, and he had a salutary effect on the public dialogue by effectively promoting conservative theory. "He made the case for markets when the case had to be made," said Democratic economist Robert Shapiro. "When we needed to talk about markets, he was on the side of history. . . . Today there is consensus among the elites on the value of markets. Nobody makes the nonmarket case anymore."

Reagan's policies in effect defunded the welfare state and made it impossible for liberals to continue creating new social programs indefinitely. For good or ill, this changed the nature of the political debate in America from how to expand the welfare state to how to restrain its growth.

Reagan also put a human face on intolerance. One of his negative legacies is that in some ways, despite his personal code of fair play, he gave public prejudice and insensitivity an air of respectability, refighting the cultural wars of the 1960s against minorities, immigrants, radicals, and others. In that sense, he unloosed some profoundly unhealthy trends in the body politic.

But at the same time, he successfully attacked the worst characteristics of the American left—especially the idea that the American role in the world was essentially corrupt. He was able to say, unabashedly and without embarrassment, that the United States was a positive force in world history, especially when compared with other great powers.

CHRONOLOGY

1911   February 6: Born in Tampico, Illinois
1920   December 6: Family moves to Dixon, Illinois
1922   June 21: Baptized into the Christian Church
1924   Autumn: Reagan enters Northside High School
1926   Spring: Takes job as a lifeguard at Lowell Park
             Begins dating Margaret Cleaver
1927   Joins Northside High School drama club
1928   Enrolls in Eureka College
1931   Wins award in the Eva Le Gallienne Competition
1932   Spring: Graduates from Eureka College, engaged
             to Margaret Cleaver
             Autumn: Becomes sports announcer for WOC in
             Davenport, Iowa
1934   Margaret Cleaver breaks off the engagement
1937   February: Reagan takes a screen test while in
             California covering the Chicago Cubs
             March 22: Signs contract with Warner Brothers
             Spring: Makes first picture—*Love Is on the Air*
             June 30: Joins SAG
1938   Meets Jane Wyman while making *Brother Rat*
             Films: *Hollywood Hotel, Swing Your Lady, Sergeant
             Murphy, Accidents Will Happen, Cowboy from Brooklyn,
             Boy Meets Girl, Girls on Probation, Brother Rat*

1939   Films: *Going Places, Secret Service of the Air,*
        Dark Victory, Code of the Secret Service, Naughty
        But Nice, Hell's Kitchen, Angels Wash Their Faces,
        Smashing the Money Ring
1940   January 26: Marries Jane Wyman at the Wee Kirk
        O'Heather Church
        Films: *Brother Rat and A Baby, An Angel from*
        Texas, Murder in the Air, Knute Rockne,
        All-American, Tugboat Annie Sails Again,
        Santa Fe Trail
1941   January 4: Birth of daughter, Maureen
        May 18: Father, Jack, dies
        July: Appointed to board of SAG
        Films: *The Bad Man, Million Dollar Baby, Nine*
        Lives Are Not Enough, International Squadron
1942   April 19: Enters Army as second lieutenant
        Films: *Kings Row, Juke Girl, Desperate Journey*
1943   Film: *This Is the Army*
1945   March 18: Wyman and Reagan adopt son Michael
1947   June: Wyman gives birth to a third child
        prematurely; the child dies the next day
        October 25: Testifies before House Un-American
        Activities Committee
        November: Elected president of SAG.
        Films: *Stallion Road, That Hagen Girl, The Voice of*
        the Turtle
1948   Wyman and Reagan divorce
1949   Films: *John Loves Mary, Night unto Night, The Girl*
        from Jones Beach, It's a Great Feeling
1950   Films: *The Hasty Heart, Louisa*
1951   Films: *Storm Warning, Bedtime for Bonzo, The Last*
        Outpost

1952	January: Leaves Warner Brothers
	March 4: Marries Nancy Davis
	October 22: Birth of Patti Reagan
	Films: *Hong Kong, She's Working Her Way Through College, The Winning Team*
1953	Films: *Tropic Zone, Law and Order*
1954	Signs contract to host "General Electric Theater"
	Films: *Prisoner of War, Cattle Queen of Montana*
1955	Film: *Tennessee's Partner*
1957	Film: *Hellcats of the Navy*
1958	May 28: Birth of Ronald Prescott Reagan
	Registers as Republican
1962	July 25: Mother, Nelle, dies
1964	October 27: Gives "The Speech" on national television in support of Republican presidential candidate Barry Goldwater
	Film: *The Killers*
1966	November: Elected governor of California over Pat Brown
1967	February 11: Faces down student protestors at the state capitol
1970	November: Wins second term as governor over Jesse Unruh
1976	August: Loses Republican presidential nomination to incumbent Gerald Ford
1980	November: Defeats incumbent Jimmy Carter to become the fortieth president of the United States
1981	January 20: Takes oath of office
	March 30: Shot by would-be assassin John Hinckley Jr.
	July 7: Nominates Sandra Day O'Connor as first woman on U.S. Supreme Court

July 29: Wins Congressional approval for tax cut
    proposal

August: Fires striking air-traffic controllers

1983   March 23: Proposes Strategic Defense Initiative

August 31: KAL flight 007 shot down by Soviet jets

October 23: Bombing of Marine barracks in Beirut

October 25: Orders invasion of Grenada

1984   November: Defeats Democratic challenger Walter
    Mondale to win second term

1985   July: Diagnosed with malignant tumor in his colon,
    which is quickly removed

November 19-21: First summit conference between
    Reagan and Mikhail Gorbachev in Geneva,
    Switzerland

1986   October 5: Eugene Hasenfus shot down over
    Nicaragua, opening up the Iran-Contra scandal

October 11-12: Second summit conference in
    Reykjavik, Iceland

1987   March 19: Reagan denies culpability in Iran-Contra

October 23: Robert Bork's nomination to the
    Supreme Court is rejected

1988   March 2: Reagan observed for possible invocation of
    Twenty-fifth Amendment

1989   January 20: Leaves White House to successor
    George Bush

1994   Reagan diagnosed with Alzheimer's disease

BIBLIOGRAPHY

I drew many of my basic perceptions and conclusions about Ronald Reagan from my experience covering the last two years of his presidency for *U.S. News & World Report*. During that time, I interviewed the president and Mrs. Reagan on several occasions, talked many times with key White House staff members and friends of the First Couple, covered countless numbers of his speeches and policy decisions, attended most of his press conferences, and traveled with him both at home and abroad. Once he left office, I stayed in contact with many intimates of the Reagans as I continued to serve as *U.S. News's* senior White House correspondent. As I researched and wrote this book, I refreshed my memory and deepened my understanding of Reagan and his era by interviewing many of these former advisers again and by adding many other sources, most of whom preferred to remain anonymous. Among the most insightful were Michael Deaver, Frank Donatelli, Marlin Fitzwater, David Gergen, and Sheila Tate.

I based some of my analysis and research on ongoing journalistic coverage of Reagan in a variety of publications, including *The New York Times* and *The Washington Post*. I found *Post* reporter Lou Cannon's book *Reagan* particularly helpful, as well as *Where's the Rest of Me?*, Reagan's first autobiography written with Richard G. Hubler, and *An American Life*, Reagan's later book.

BOOKS

Barber, James David. *The Presidential Character: Predicting Performance in the White House.* Englewood Cliffs, N.J.: Prentice Hall, 1985.

Boyarsky, Bill. *Ronald Reagan: His Life and Rise to the Presidency.* New York: Random House, 1981.

Cannon, Lou. *Reagan.* New York: G.P. Putnam's Sons, 1982.

———— *Ronald Reagan: The Role of a Lifetime.* New York: Simon & Schuster, 1991.

Edwards, Anne. *Early Reagan.* New York: William Morrow, 1987.

Fitzwater, Marlin. *Call the Briefing!* New York: Times Books, 1995.

Goldman, Peter, and Tony Fuller. *The Quest for the Presidency 1984.* New York: Bantam Books, 1985.

Leamer, Laurence. *Make-Believe.* New York: Harper & Row, 1983.

Lewis, Tom. *Empire of the Air.* New York: HarperCollins, 1991.

Meyer, Jane, and Doyle McManus. *Landslide: The Unmaking of the President 1984–1988.* Boston: Houghton Mifflin, 1988.

Miroff, Bruce. "The Presidency and the Public: Leadership as Spectacle" in Michael Nelson, ed., "The Presidency and the Political System." *Congressional Quarterly,* Washington, D.C., 1995.

Nelson, Michael, ed., "The Presidency A to Z." *Congressional Quarterly,* Washington, D.C., 1992.

Nevins, Allan, and Henry Steele Commager. *A Pocket History of the United States.* New York: Pocket Books, 1976.

Oberdorfer, Don. *The Turn: From the Cold War to a New Era, The United States and the Soviet Union, 1983–1990.* New York: Poseidon Press, 1991.

Quick, Lawrence J. *Jane Wyman: The Actress and the Woman.* New York: Delacorte, 1986.

Reagan, Nancy, with William Novak. *My Turn: The Memoirs of Nancy Reagan.* New York: Random House, 1989.

Reagan, Ronald. *An American Life.* New York: Simon & Schuster, 1990.

Reagan, Ronald with Richard G. Hubler. *Where's the Rest of Me?* New York: Duell, Sloan and Pearce, 1965.

Smith, Hedrick, Adam Clymer, Robert Lindsey, Richard Burt, and Leonard Silk. *Reagan: The Man, the President.* New York: Macmillan, 1980.

Speakes, Larry, with Robert Pack. *Speaking Out.* New York: Charles Scribner's Sons, 1988.

Walsh, Kenneth T. *Feeding the Beast: The White House Versus the Press.* New York: Random House, 1996.

Wills, Garry. *Reagan's America.* New York: Penguin Books, 1988

SOURCES

CHAPTER ONE: Middle American

REFERENCES

Boyarsky; Cannon; Edwards; Lewis; Nevins and Commager; Reagan; Reagan with Hubler; Wills; *Washington Post.*

SOURCES

p. 3 *"Reagan's father"*: Reagan with Hubler, p. 3.

p. 4 *"Jack Reagan moved his wife"*: Cannon, pp. 24–25.

p. 4 *"Ronald recalls in his autobiography"*: Reagan with Hubler, p. 7.

p. 5 *"Nelle Reagan was Scots-Irish"*: ibid, p. 9.

p. 6 *"Many folks reasoned"*: ibid, p. 23.

p. 6 *"All men were created "*: Boyarsky, p. 25.

p. 6 *"Jack forbade his sons"*: Recounted in several biographies, including Boyarsky, p. 32.

p. 7 *"I'm a sucker for hero worship,"*: Cannon, pp. 18–19.

p. 7 *"[M]y reading"*: Reagan, p. 32.

p. 8 *"[T]he right is more"*: Nevins and Commager, pp. 395–96.

p. 8 *"I think the realization"*: Reagan, p. 26.

p. 11 *"Heroes are more fun"*: Reagan with Hubler, p. 38.

p. 12 *"Lifeguarding provides"* and ensuing: Reagan with Hubler, pp. 20–21.

p. 13 *"It is the last"*: Cannon, pp. 28–29.

p. 13 *"As far as I am"*: *Washington Post*, Oct. 19, 1982.

p. 14 *"Eureka—Greek for 'I have found it' "*: Reagan, p. 46.

p. 15 *"Not once did we"*: Reagan with Hubler, pp. 29–30.

p. 15 *"Giving that speech"*: Reagan, p. 48.

p. 17 *"Didn't even blink"*: Reagan with Hubler, pp. 63–64.

p. 18 *"Government giveaway"*: Reagan, p. 67.

p. 18 *"Reagan emerged"*: Cannon, pp. 31–32.

p. 20 *"No actor can ask"*: Reagan with Hubler, p. 43.

CHAPTER TWO: Actor
REFERENCES

Boyarsky; Cannon; Edwards; Nelson; Quick; Reagan; Reagan with Hubler; Wills.

SOURCES

p. 26 *"Warner's offer contract"*: Reagan, p. 81.

p. 26 *"It would be the start"*: Nelson, p. 362.

p. 26 *"Reagan's photographic memory"*: Cannon, p. 53.

p. 28 *"I was still a Midwest movie fan"*: Reagan with Hubler, pp. 87-88.

p. 28 *"the publicity department"*: ibid.

p. 31 *"A nearly perfect part"*: ibid, p. 93.

p. 31 *"Reagan's performance in* Knute Rockne, All American*"*: Edwards, p. 214.

p. 31 *"So much of our profession"*: Reagan with Hubler, p. 6.

p. 32 *"We've kept a little"*: ibid, pp. 294–95

p. 33 *"I think the first"*: ibid, pp. 123–24.

p. 33 *"If I suggested"*: Reagan, p. 102.

p. 36 *"I knew little and cared less"*: Reagan with Hubler, pp. 138–39.

p. 36 *"According to some historians"*: Cannon, pp. 74–75.

p. 37 *"Communist infiltration"*: ibid, p. 76.

p. 40 *"As historian Garry Wills reports"*: Wills, pp. 248–50.

p. 40 *"I heard whispers"*: Reagan, p. 115.

p. 41 *"The Reds know"*: Quoted in Boyarsky, pp. 65–66.

CHAPTER THREE: Ideologue
REFERENCES

Boyarsky; Nancy Reagan with Novak; Wills.

SOURCES

p. 45 *"It was nineteenth"*: Wills, p. 319.

p. 46 *"A joke made the rounds"*: Boyarsky, p. 78.

p. 47 *"It was now his professional duty"*: Wills, pp. 332–33.

p. 48–49 *"The Speech has been reported in many sources"* Quoted in Boyarsky, p.79

p. 50 *"socialized medicare"* and ensuing: Wills, p. 334

p. 52 *"It is the post-World War II California"*: Boyarsky, p. 13.

p. 55 *"Nancy Davis made eleven movies"*: Wills, pp 214–17.

p. 55 *"She cared for her husband"*: Nancy Reagan with Novak, pp. 76–77.

p. 55 *"My life didn't"*: ibid, p. 93.

p. 56 *"Nelle never saw anything evil"*: ibid, pp. 107–108.

p. 58 *"He would say that coming home to Nancy"*: ibid, pp. 121–23.

p. 58 *"Reagan's political transformation"*: Cannon, pp. 96–97.

p. 59 *"This superstructure of government"*: Quoted in Boyarsky, pp. 78–79. Boyarsky is among many writers, including historian Garry Wills and journalist Lou Cannon, who give similar accounts of Reagan's philosophy as outlined in his speeches.

CHAPTER FOUR: Politician

REFERENCES

Barber; Boyarsky; Cannon; Smith, Clymer, et al; Wills.

SOURCES

p. 62 *"Stuart Spencer and Bill Roberts"*: Wills, pp. 350–52.

p. 62 *"He took it all"*: ibid, p. 354.

p. 64 *"The tower of Jell-O"*: Cannon, p. 111.

p. 64 *"failed leadership"*: Reported by many sources.

p. 64 *"Observe the rules"*: Cannon, pp. 113–14 .

p. 64 *"I'm running against"*: Reported in many sources.

p. 65 *"I could take some"*: Quoted in Cannon, p. 120

p. 66 *"In January 1965"*: This account of how the millionaires settled on Reagan is recounted by Cannon, pp. 103–104.

p. 66 *"Reagan is the man"* and ensuing: Barber, p. 481.

p. 66 *"We believed"*: Smith, Clymer et al, p. 37.

p. 66 *"We checked with people"*: ibid, p. 37.

p. 67 *"Ronald Reagan materialized"*: Quoted in Barber, p. 482.

p. 68 *"Clark would develop:"* Cannon, p. 125.

p. 68 *"On March 28, Smith presented the legislature"*: ibid, p. 127.

p. 68 *"On June 13, 1967, Reagan signed a bill"*: ibid, pp. 130–31.

p. 69 *"A tree is a tree"*: Reported by many sources.

p. 70 *"During his administration"*: Boyarsky, pp. 166–67.

p. 70 *"State government should intercede"*: Boyarsky, p. 175.

p. 71 *"Ladies and gentlemen"*: Cannon, p. 150.

p. 72 *"At one point in February 1969"*: ibid, pp. 151–52.

p. 76 *"The greatest domestic"*: Reported in many sources.

p. 77 *"Money is the mother's"*: ibid.

p. 78 *"Strengthen family"*: ibid.

p. 78 *"We simply cannot"*: Reported in many sources.

p. 79 *"Under Reagan"*: Reagan's record is discussed in considerable detail in Cannon, pp. 184–85.

p. 80 *"We in our party"*: Discussed in Cannon, p. 188.

p. 81 *"Biographer Lou Cannon estimates"*: Cannon, p. 196.

p. 81 *"Raising the banner"*: Quoted in Cannon, p. 197.

p. 83 *"We bought it,"*: Author's observation.

p. 84 *"In the end"*: Cannon, p. 225.

p. 85 *"Turn Mr. Reagan's"*: Author's observation.

p. 87 *"Are you better"*: Author's observation.

p. 87 *"Would you laugh"*: Cannon, p. 306.

p. 88 *"I bet there's"*: Cannon, p. 303.

p. 89 *"By the time Reagan reached"*: Barber, p. 490.

CHAPTER FIVE: President: First Term

REFERENCES

Barber; Cannon, *Ronald Reagan, Ronald Reagan: Role of a Lifetime*; Goldman and Fuller; Miroff; Oberdorfer; Reagan; Smith, Clymer et al; Walsh.

SOURCES

p. 91 *"We have every right"*: Author's observation.

p. 92 *"minor-league"*: Cannon, p. 71.

p. 92 " *Reagan was the first*": Author's interview with Michael Deaver.

p. 93 *"You know"*: ibid.

p. 93 *"President Washington"* and ensuing: Reported in many sources.

p. 94 *"Reagan sits at any gathering"*: Quoted in Smith et al., p. 169.

p. 97 *"On March 30, 1981"*: Cannon, pp. 402–404.

p. 98 *"He believed"*: Author's interview with Michael Deaver.

p. 99 *"Please tell me"*: Reported in many sources.

p. 99 *"God saved me"*: Author's interview.

p. 100 *"a tough, determined president"*: Miroff, pp. 278–79.

p. 101 *"That debate will not take"*: Goldman and Fuller, p. 20.

p. 101 *"I'm getting the shit"*: Cannon: *Ronald Reagan: Role of a Lifetime*, p. 116.

p. 101 *"Inflation had slowed"*: Barber, pp. 460–61.

p. 102 *"Meanwhile, the Reagan administration"*: Barber, p. 460.

p. 102 *"Economist Robert Reich"*: Barber, p. 460.

p. 103 *"He's cutting the heart"*: Cannon: *Ronald Reagan: Role of a Lifetime*, p. 116.

p. 106 *"One Reagan is the rhetorical"*: Smith, Clymer et al., pp. 98–99.

p. 107 *"World War II"*: ibid, p. 100.

p. 107 *"The Soviet Union"* : ibid.

p. 108 For a more detailed account of the Grenada episode, see Miroff, pp. 284–87.

p. 109 *"A brutal group"* and ensuing: Reported in many sources.

p. 111 *"massacre"* and ensuing: Reported in many sources.

p. 111 *"We may not be able"*: Quoted in Oberdorfer, p. 62.

p. 112 *"Only 35 percent"*: Goldman and Fuller, pp. 20–21.

p. 113 *"Ronald Reagan used to"*: Walsh, p. 40. This discussion of Reagan's media strategy is based largely on research Walsh conducted for *Feeding the Beast: The White House Versus the Press*, Random House, New York, 1996.

p. 114 *"Powerful, intimate, uncontrolled"*: Goldman and Fuller, p. 29.

p. 114 *"The modern presidency"*: Barber, p. 493.

p. 115 *"Give Mr. Reagan a good script"*: Quoted in Barber, p. 493.

p. 115 *"Certain elements"*: Cannon, pp. 88–89.

p. 116 *"One day, Deaver came into"*: Recounted by author in *Feeding the Beast: The White House Versus the Press,* Random House, New York, 1996, p. 41.

p. 121 *"substantive record"*: Goldman and Fuller, p. 246.

p. 121 *"paint Mondale as"*: Goldman and Fuller, ibid., p. 247.

p. 122 *"My fellow Americans"*: Reported in many sources.

CHAPTER SIX: President: Second Term
REFERENCES

Fitzwater; Mayer and McManus; Miroff; Oberdorfer; Nancy Reagan with Novak; Ronald Reagan with Hubler; Speakes with Pack; Wills.

SOURCES

p. 126 *"Even today"*: Fitzwater, pp. 129–30.

p. 127 *"In the summit meetings"*: Fitzwater, pp. 130–31.

p. 127 *"I think we must"* and ensuing: Interview with *U.S. News.*

p. 128 *"Ronald Reagan's main"*: Interview with *U.S. News.*

p. 129 *"Since the dawn"*: Reagan, p. 633.

p. 130 *"Since Richard Nixon's first summit meeting"*: ibid, pp. 107–108.

p. 131 *"He proposed an indefinite"*: Oberdorfer, pp. 114–15.

p. 131 *"You have taught"*: Author's interview with Michael Deaver

p. 131 *"Negotiations would sometimes"*: Quoted in Speakes with Pack, "Speaking Out," p. 125.

p. 132 *"You and I were born in small towns"*: Quoted in Oberdorfer.

p. 133 *"The president explained"*: Speakes with Pack, pp. 137–38.

p. 133 *"I can't believe"*: Quoted in Speakes with Pack, p. 134.

p. 134 *"We've seen what"*: ibid., pp. 138–39.

p. 134 *"We sat in a room"*: ibid, pp. 138–39.

p. 134 *"When the two men met on October 11–12, 1986"*: ibid., pp. 145–47.

p. 135 *"When the two men walked out of Hofdi House"*: ibid., p. 143.

p. 135 *"I better go"*: Recounted in Fitzwater, p. 148.

p. 137 *"This is a real man"*: The story of the 1,200-pound man is described in Fitzwater, pp. 151–52.

p. 137 *"I know Gorbachev"*: ibid.

p. 138 *"Look at that"*: Author's observation.

p. 139 *"I didn't have cancer"*: Quoted in Speakes with Pack, p. 192.

p. 139 *"The first photograph"*: ibid, p. 194.

p. 143 *"I made a very"* and ensuing: Reported in many sources.

p. 145 *"he used a prime-time press conference"*: Fitzwater, pp. 109–14.

p. 146 *"...Reagan's great strength"*: ibid, p. 117.

p. 146 *"He did not provide"*: ibid, p. 119.

p. 149 Described, among other places, in Garry Wills, p. 227

p. 150 *"After spending the better part"*: Mayer and McManus,
pp. vii–xi. As a White House correspondent for *U.S. News* during
this period, my sources gave much the same account.

p. 150 *"The next morning, March 2"*: Mayer and McManus, ibid., p. xi.

p. 150 *"They had argued"*: Fitzwater, p. 79.

p. 151 *"They did not like"*: Fitzwater, p. 140.

p. 153 *"I wasn't in that movie"*: Author's interview.

CHAPTER SEVEN: Reagan's Legacy
REFERENCES
Miroff; Ronald Reagan with Hubler; Nancy Reagan with Novak.
SOURCES

p. 156 *"You and I have rendezvous"*: Quoted in Reagan with Hubler, p. 312.

p. 156 *"Ronnie didn't seek the presidency"*: Nancy Reagan with Novak,
p. 113.

p. 158 *"The only time"*: Author's interview with Gary Bauer.

p. 159 *"Ronald Reagan is the touchstone"*: Donatelli, ibid.

p. 159 *"the father of the modern"*: Author's interview with Frank
Donatelli.

p. 159 *"The Reagan presidency was a triumph"*: Miroff, pp. 281–82.

p. 163 *"He made the case"*: Author's interview with Robert Shapiro.

INDEX

ACKNOWLEDGMENTS

I gratefully acknowledge the many friends, advisers, and critics of Ronald and Nancy Reagan who provided their insights and cooperation in the writing of this book.

I owe particular thanks to the Reagans themselves and to former president George Bush and Barbara Bush. I interviewed each of them several times while covering the White House for *U.S. News & World Report*, and those experiences were extremely helpful in informing my subsequent research. Thanks also to Roger Ailes, the late Lee Atwater, Howard Baker, Gary Bauer, Frank Carlucci, Elaine Crispen, A.B. Culvahouse, Mitch Daniels, Mike Deaver, Frank Donatelli, Ken Duberstein, Marlin Fitzwater, Craig Fuller, David Gergen, Tom Griscom, Dan Howard, Jim Lake, Jim Pinkerton, Roman Popadiuk, Colin Powell, Donald Regan, Sheila Tate, Dennis Thomas, and Richard Wirthlin.

I also want to thank a variety of others not associated with the Reagans who helped shape my thinking about the former president and his era. They include Michael Beschloss, Lou Cannon, Tom Cronin, Don Foley, Al From, Geoff Garin, Stan Greenberg, Harrison Hickman, Wil Marshall, Rob Shapiro, and John Walcott.

My thanks to Joe Spieler, my agent, and to Tom Dyja for his deft editing of this manuscript.

ABOUT THE AUTHOR

Kenneth T. Walsh has covered the presidency for *U.S. News & World Report* since 1986. He is the winner of the two most prestigious awards for covering the White House, the Aldo Beckman Award and the Gerald R. Ford Prize, and is the former president of the White House Correspondents' Association. He is an adjunct professor of communication at the American University in Washington.